Drink and Drug

Drink and Drugs at Work

The Consuming Problem

Fred Dickenson

Institute of Personnel Management

First published 1988

Phototypeset by James Jenkins Typesetting (Wandsworth) and printed in Great Britain by Dotesios Printers Ltd. Bradford-on-Avon, Wiltshire.

British Library Cataloguing in Publication Data
Dickenson, Fred
Drink and drugs at work.
1. Great Britain. Personnel. Alcoholism & drug abuse
I. Title
658.3'822

ISBN 0-85292-410-0

Contents

Acknowledgements vi

Introduction 1

1 The Background 3
2 The Nature of the Problem 12
3 Alcohol and Drugs Policies 22
4 Implementing an Alcohol and Drugs Policy 30
5 The Law and Alcohol and Drugs in the Workplace 43
6 The Personnel Implications 67

Appendix 1
Substance Misuse at Work: An IPM Guide 83

Appendix 2
Alcohol and Drugs Policy: An Example 95

Appendix 3
Examples of Company Policies 99

Appendix 4
Case Studies 119

Appendix 5
Guide to Drug Types 125

Appendix 6
Organizations dealing with Alcohol and Drug Misuse 128

Appendix 7
References and Bibliography 129

Acknowledgements

This publication has been prepared by a working party of the Institute of Personnel Management's National Committee on Pay and Employment Conditions. The members of the working party were as follows:

Fred Dickenson, Personnel Consultant, The Save the Children Fund, on secondment from IBM United Kingdom Ltd.
Coilin O'Broin, Coilin O'Broin and Associates
Peter Richards, Senior Personnel Manager, The Royal Bank of Scotland
Margaret Wright, Senior Personnel Officer, British Gas (Scotland)
Steve Palmer, Manager – Pay and Employment Conditions, IPM
Matthew Reisz, Commissioning Editor, IPM

Assistance with the project was also given by **Steve Turley,** Personnel Manager, Burmah Oil Trading.

The working party recognizes with deep gratitude the major input of the two co-opted members: **Ossie O'Brien,** Director of the Workplace Advisory Service, Alcohol Concern, and **Hugh Dufficy,** Deputy Director of the Standing Conference on Drug Abuse, who was assisted by Rosemary Morle. On these two members fell a great deal of the preparation of the technical chapters of this guide. Without their assistance this project would have been considerably more difficult if not impossible. Considerable thanks are also due to **Alan Bensted** of Bristol Polytechnic who prepared Chapter 5 on the legal aspects of substance abuse at work. The working party would also like to place on record their thanks to **Erica Reeve** who, as an IPM student at Kingston Polytechnic, undertook a project analysing organizations' alcohol policies. Her work was the starting point for this project.

Finally, but not least, it remains to thank very much the many people who answered our request for help by providing policies, guidance and advice, and who gave of their time so freely.

Throughout, and notwithstanding this help, this has remained an IPM publication. Any faults that exist, therefore, are unequivocally ours.

Introduction

The aim of this book is to provide personnel managers with a practical guide to establishing workplace policies on alcohol and drugs. It has been commissioned by the Institute of Personnel Management in response to a growing awareness of the extent of such problems within the workplace and the need to take action to reduce them.

In every chapter of this book apart from the one on the law, we have veered away from the use of pejorative terms such as 'alcoholics' or 'drug addicts'. We feel that such terms only serve to confuse the subject rather than assist in its clarification. In the main, we have used 'alcohol abuse' or 'drug misuse', although the reader will also find references to alcohol and drug-related problems, excessive drinking, heavy drinkers, and inappropriate drinking. These terms are defined by the context in which they are used and relate to the possible adverse impact on the workplace of the problematic use of alcohol and drugs. Basically, problematic use can be divided into three main but not mutually exclusive areas:

Inappropriate use may aggravate an existing unhappy or difficult condition which it was intended to ameliorate. It may impair social functioning. At work, the resulting intoxication may lead to the impairment of relationships with colleagues, and an inability to perform necessary tasks satisfactorily. It may bring the individual into conflict with the disciplinary procedures and possibly the law.

Habitual use may make the individual so dependent on the effects of a drug that the desire for these effects becomes a central and overriding concern of their daily life. Dependence is perhaps the most difficult type of drug problem. It may most usefully be described as a way of living in the world by psychologically shielding oneself from it. This shield and the habitual use of drugs may become destructive in a variety of ways to the drug-dependent person and to those who share in his or her life. A habitual drug user will almost certainly function at work at less than an optimum level of efficiency and is more likely to be accident and sickness prone than others.

Excessive use may lead to 'poisoning' in the form of physical or psychological ill health. It may lead to accidents and, in the end, may be fatal.

To assist the reader in knowing more about alcohol and drug use and their associated problems, this book draws together some background information on a range of issues. Case studies which may prove useful for training purposes are included in Appendix 4 and the new IPM guide to the issue, launched at the same time as this book, is included in full as Appendix 1. The first sections of Chapters 1 and 2 deal with alcohol, the second with illicit drug use. This separation reflects the confusion that exists in our society regarding the discussion of drugs. It could be argued that they are all drugs and therefore should be treated together. However, the legal process does make a distinction and we have followed that protocol. Nevertheless, in discussing industry's response to alcohol and drug problems, we have reunited the themes as we see these as one.

In researching the material for this book, it has become clear to us that there is little constructive data on the effect of drug use on industry. The available material relates primarily to the United States, which has a different sociological structure and offers a different choice of drugs to users. What we do know is that the number of people who are in full-time employment and seek help for drug-related problems suggests that, as with alcohol, industry needs to consider the matter seriously.

It is hoped that this book will encourage that serious consideration and that it will enable personnel managers and others to construct realistic policies which can be practically applied at the workplace.

Ossie O'Brien
Hugh Dufficy

Chapter One
The Background

Ossie O'Brien and Hugh Dufficy

Alcohol

Alcohol has been consumed almost throughout human history. In Stone Age societies it was used as a drug, a food and a medicine. References to it can be found in the Bible and in the ancient writings of India, Persia, Greece, Rome and Egypt. As early as 2000 BC in China it was found necessary to have rules about the sale of alcohol. The persistence and spread of its use throughout the ages suggest that alcohol has probably always been associated with pleasure.

Myths

Certainly, today, it is the pleasure rather than the harm associated with alcohol that is uppermost in the minds of people. More than 90 per cent of the population drinks, most without any apparent harm. Consequently, myths about it still abound. Everyone has come across them, perhaps even believed them. Because for some people alcohol can be a social lubricant, liberating the shy and the tense, it is seen as a harmless stimulant, an indispensable part of human sociability. It is thought to be nutritious because people who drink considerable amounts put on weight. In the past doctors have sometimes prescribed a tot or two for their patients, so it is endowed by some with medicinal powers. Cold people, especially the elderly, are sometimes given alcohol to warm them through, so it can stave off hypothermia. Car drivers boast that they can drive better after a couple of drinks, so what is all the fuss about stiffer drink/drive laws?

Of course alcohol has some beneficial qualities but not usually the ones popularly supposed. It can facilitate social ease but it does so in a way rarely understood, It is a depressant not a stimulant. A psychoactive drug which depresses those parts of the brain normally controlling the social and personal rules of behaviour. That is why shy people often become more talkative and gregarious. Alcohol depresses their inhibitions. (*NB.* Sometimes alcohol simply reinforces the pre-existing state.)

As for its food value, it is true that alcohol contains calories and provides energy. But it cannot be stored and contains no protein, no fats and no vitamins. Hence the paradox of the well-caloried corpulent drinker who is really undernourished. Equally the warming-up effect is something of an illusion. Alcohol increases the size of the blood vessels on the body surface, which gives the skin a warm sensation. But it actually lowers body temperature. Medicinally, it is probably true that its only beneficial value is psychosomatic. Tentative claims have been made that it can help people at risk from heart attacks by causing the blood vessels of the heart wall to dilate. Most authorities regard the claim sceptically. Road accident statistics give the lie to the claimed improved driving skills of the inebriated.

Perhaps the biggest myth of all is that it is only other people who will ever suffer from alcohol-related problems. Drinks trade spokespersons and individuals in the community take refuge in the official statistics. For England and Wales these vary from the DHSS figure of 500,000 in 1976 to 740,000 from OPCS in 1977 and the 890,000 from the Office of Health Economics. Add in estimates for Scotland and Northern Ireland and we have a range of 600,000 to 1 million problem drinkers in the United Kingdom. This is only 1.7 per cent to 2.2 per cent of the over-15 population, which is reassuringly low for the complacent or vested interests. But it is only part of the story.

Consequences

Excessive drinking at some point in a person's life is known to be much more common than the official statistics reveal. American research suggests that, if a lifetime view of Britain's post-war generation is taken, 1 in 6 (17 per cent) run the risk of encountering an alcohol problem at some stage. Around 25 per cent of all British men can be expected to experience trouble at some point in their lives *(The Drinking Revolution* 1987).

This trouble can take a variety of forms, depending on the levels and time scale of the drinking. Excessive drinking over a long period can lead to severe physical and mental illness. Each year there are close on 3000 deaths from cirrhosis of the liver and in a similar period 17,000 admissions to psychiatric hospitals and units are connected with alcohol misuse.

The statistics (gathered from a variety of sources and for various years) for other alcohol-related incidents are horrendous. A few examples will suffice: up to 62 per cent of serious head injuries; 66 per cent of suicide attempts and deaths; 20.5 per cent of cases of child abuse; 45 per cent of cases of wounding or assault; 48 per cent of fatal road accidents to young people and 25 per cent of all deaths in road accidents are associated with drinking and driving (*Alcohol Concern Factsheet* 1988).

In terms of personal illness problem drinking is as widespread a health hazard as cancer and more than twice as common as diabetes or chronic bronchitis. It is the third biggest killer after cancer and chronic heart disease. All these factors involve costs for society. The work of Professsor Alan Maynard, Director of the Centre for Health Economics at York University, suggests that the social cost of alcohol misuse in Britain in 1987 prices would be close on £2 billion a year. He has made clear that this is a conservative estimate (McDonnell and Maynard 1985).

Favourite drug

As evidence that alcohol is the United Kingdom's favourite drug £16,474 million was spent on it in 1986. At just over 5 per cent that is not much different from the proportion of GDP spent on Defence, Education, or the National Health Service (CSO 1988). It really is big business. The brewing and related industries employed almost one million people in 1986, about 3 per cent of the total workforce (CSO 1988).

The Exchequer benefits too. In 1985-6 taxes on alcohol brought in £6,351 million, more than £17 million a day (Brewers' Society 1986). It contributed around 6 per cent to total income from taxes and 11 per cent of all taxes on expenditure. There is also a net gain to the balance of payments. In 1986 exports were worth £1,331.7 million, a quarter as much again as the cost of imports at £1,008.3 million (CSO 1988). More than 80 per cent of Scotch whisky is exported. So it might be argued that the economic benefits far outweigh the social costs and therefore there is nothing to worry about.

Apart from the fact that the costs are probably underestimated it should not be the case in a civilized society that figures count more than people. That is why it is important for alcohol misuse to be regarded seriously and proper provision made for preventive education and adequate and widespread treatment services to pick up the casualties. In any case the increased costs from more alcohol education and improved services may well be offset by the economic gains derived from a healthier, better adjusted, more law-abiding and more efficient society.

Role of government

To achieve this it would be necessary to effect a significant reduction in the United Kingdom's consumption of alcohol. Recently there has been a slight shift downwards in per capita consumption but at 7 litres per year in 1985-6 it was still almost double the 1949-50 figure of 3.7 litres (Brewers' Society 1986). A major fall will only come about through a combination of preventive education and direct government action. The government's role was recognized in a 1979 Government Think Tank report titled *Alcohol Policies* (Central Policy Review Staff 1979) (unpublished, except in Sweden). The report suggested that all the government departments involved in alcohol-related matters should be brought together to establish a policy for action.

Immediate changes recommended included increases in excise duties in line with inflation, stricter enforcement of the law on under-age drinking, a workplace alcohol programme led by the Government as a major employer, tougher drinking and driving legislation, and the setting up of an advisory council on alcohol policies to encourage and monitor action.

Nothing much happened except that in 1982 the DHSS published a policy report, *Drinking Sensibly,* which played down many of the Think Tank's recommendations. However, during 1988, an inter-departmental ministerial group set up in September 1987 to co-ordinate government policy returned to some of them. For example, in July 1988 the group, known as the Wakeham Committee after its chairman, asked the Department of Employment to take up with the CBI and the TUC the need for workplace alcohol policies. Time will tell whether this heralds a change towards more positive ways of dealing with alcohol-related problems at work.

Preventive paradox

Of course, not everything can be achieved by government. However, macro-level activity either by government or national agencies, or both, is important, especially because of what is known as the preventive paradox (Kreitman 1986). The paradox is that the social groups most at risk constitute only a small proportion of the total harm. For example, in a survey of Scottish drinking habits, it was found that among working-class men, those aged 17-30 years were three times more likely to be heavy drinkers than the over-30s. But there were three times as many men in the older age group. So, although much less at risk, the older men contributed just as many heavy drinkers (Dight 1976).

In another study, of women's drinking, it was found that young unmarried women, aged 18-24, were more than four times as likely as 30-54 year-old married women to drink over 20 units a week. However, the older group, because of its larger size, contributes just as many heavy drinkers (Breeze 1985). Consequently, concentrating policy and resources on particular groups of heavy drinkers is of limited value. Public education aimed at encouraging everyone to drink less might achieve more, partly because the habits of moderate drinkers are probably more easily influenced. There is not much doubt that most people would benefit from drinking less.

Safe Limits

The evidence is increasing that there are substantial risks among men who drink more than 21 units a week (10½ pints of ordinary strength beer, 21 whiskies or 21 sherries or 21 glasses of wine) and women who drink more than 14 units a week (7 pints of ordinary strength beer or 14 whiskies or 14 sherries or 14 glasses of wine). As a result the major alcohol agencies, Alcohol Concern, the Health Education Authority and the royal medical colleges, now agree that 21 units and 14 units are the safe weekly limits for men and women respectively. The risk of getting into serious trouble from alcohol is significantly increased between 14 and 21 units for women and 21-35 units for men. These are standard pub measures and not the usually more generous measures poured at home All drinks carry the same kind of alcohol and one type of drink is no safer than another. All can harm the individual drinker as well as others.

Drug Use

The preceding section, concerning alcohol, concentrated on dispelling popular misconceptions about its effects and costs both on an individual and social level. Complacency within our society about the effects of alcohol have distorted our view of its potential harm.

In respect of 'drug misuse' the opposite is true. Most people would be forgiven for believing that once a person has used an illegal drug, eg cannabis, they are on the slippery slope. It is only necessary to look at the reporting in the media of drug use, over the past thirty years, to understand why these myths have developed.

Drug use, as with alcohol, has a long-established history within our society. The use of drugs is universal and encompasses many aspects of our social institutions. The use of drugs can be found in religious ceremonies, recreational activities and obviously in medicine. It is only in the past one-hundred years that legislation has been introduced to try to limit or restrict the use of drugs. Eminent figures from a variety of spheres have used drugs for pleasure, and more importantly have lived to tell the tale. Freud and his use of cocaine and Coleridge and his use of opium are both examples of how the intelligentsia indulged in drug use.

With the emergence of a youth culture in the 1950s and the increasing interest among some young people in seeking new pleasures and challenges, drug use was no longer confined to the intelligentsia. Naturally this caused concern among the older population who found the constant questioning and challenging of their views a burden and an irritation. Drugs became linked to young people's disaffection with the status quo and thus heralded a new wave of reaction against them.

The choice of drugs available to young people increased dramatically as technological advances enabled science to create new medicines. The 1950s saw LSD enter the market. It was heralded as the new wonder drug in the treatment of psychological disorders. It soon found its way into the recreational use of the young. Many other substances have been produced, primarily for medical purposes but, as with LSD, have been put to a recreational purpose by young people.

As the variety of drugs consumed for pleasure increased, so social attitudes became increasingly confused. Alcohol and tobacco are the most common drugs of choice for pleasure in our society and have remained to some degree socially acceptable. The term misuse is rarely given to them unless the individual concerned is physically harmed by their consumption. Illicit drugs on the other hand are constantly termed as being misused, irrespective of the harm or lack of it to the individual. By lumping together all forms of illegal drug use – eg heroin, LSD, cannabis – we lose sight of the actual effects of the individual drugs, opting instead to take the worst scenario as the inevitable outcome of all use. A result of this process is the idea that, once an illicit substance is used, irrespective of how mild it might be, the user is on a slippery slope.

It is only by looking at the way in which drugs become problems for individuals that we can start to draw conclusions as to the real nature of drug misuse. Agencies working with people who have identified themselves as having problems with drug taking have come to the conclusion that perhaps, as with alcohol, use only becomes a problem when it is used to cope with difficult social, psychological, economic or physical difficulties, or where an individual has unknowingly become physically dependent.

In order to combat the consumption of drugs for purposes other than medical, a series of legislation was passed by parliament. The culmination of this legislation can be found in the Misuse of Drugs Act 1971. The Act categorized drugs into Class A, Class B and Class C. Medical practitioners were required by this law to notify the Home Office if they treated a patient whom they knew or suspected was addicted to certain named natural or synthetic opiates or cocaine. The Home Office record is the only national statistic available to us to measure the number of people using drugs. These figures bear little resemblance to the actual number of illicit drug users, as few people seek medical help for problems with drugs and doctors are not required to notify those using drugs other than notifiable ones.

The Home Office accepts that a more accurate figure of drug users can be obtained by multiplying their figures by five. It is difficult to estimate the numbers of people who are using other, non-notifiable drugs. Research estimates on cannabis use alone would sugest that 30 per cent of the under-40s have used it at one time or other.

People from all classes, both genders and all ethnic backgrounds use drugs. Many of these will be in full-time employment. Research carried out among drugs agencies has shown that between a quarter and a half of those with a problem attending for help were in employment. Given that only one in ten approach services for treatment there is every reason for employers to acknowledge that they may have a drug-using employee.

How best then to deal with the problem of drug use within the workplace? If a punitive line is followed, there is a danger of alienating the user, thus forcing them into secrecy. According to SCODA, the current political campaign known as 'the war on drugs' could be having just that effect. Hence the low numbers of people attending services for help. A war on drugs is interpreted by the user as a war, not on the individual drug consumed, but rather on them as users of such drugs. Morally, many people may agree with this approach. However, it is necessary to look further if there is to be an effective prevention of the kinds of problems that drug use can cause for the individual and subsequently society as a whole.

If people are to come forward for help with any problem they have it is important that two conditions exist. First, the person offering help must understand the drug user's position and potential problem. Secondly, users must be enabled to seek appropriate solutions to their problems. If the drug users are cast in the role of the enemy it becomes difficult if not impossible to convince them that they will receive appropriate help. This does not condone drug use but is an attempt to recognize that those who choose drug use as an option are not inherently evil but that, when in difficulties, they need understanding of their problem, and assistance to overcome those difficulties.

In anticipation of there being such a problem within the workforce it makes sense for employers to consider the implementation of a drugs policy. The framework for such a policy should concentrate on those people whose work is affected by their drug use. It should be clear and non-punitive for, as has been demonstrated, a punitive approach will only force people into secrecy and fail to address the real problem.

Having explained the main difficulties of discussing drug use and the confusion that exists around the issue, there is a final dilemma of HIV infection and AIDS. Over the past few years as more has been discovered about the transmission of HIV, the virus which precipitates the onset of AIDS in one in ten of those affected, the link between injecting drugs and the transmission of HIV has been recognized. Drugs are not always injected, but are more commonly snorted or smoked. If a drug user does inject it is imperative that they do not share their equipment and that they sterilize the equipment after every use. Through media coverage the non-drug-using population may be under the impression that all people who use drugs are potentially spreaders of the virus. This is untrue. The emphasis on explaining the HIV/AIDS issue has been placed on blaming groups of people rather than looking at its transmission. It is currently being suggested that drugs users form the bridging group to the wider heterosexual community. This is an erroneous way of looking at the issue which only seeks to alienate drug users rather than educate the population at large on the modes of transmission. The link between drug use and HIV infection could pose a problem for employers and disputes may arise through ignorance, with refusals to work alongside individuals who have been identified as drug users, and subsequently been seen as possible 'AIDS carriers'. Whilst this is not the right place to discuss setting up policies around HIV/AIDS, it is essential that those responsible for staff welfare are aware of this problem. Such awareness can help to pre-empt potential conflict through appropriate education. The responsibility the whole population has to regulate its behaviour in order to avoid contracting or passing on the virus must not be overlooked.

Chapter Two

The Nature of the Problem

Ossie O'Brien and Hugh Dufficy

Alcohol

A widespread problem

Alcohol misuse is often thought to be confined to a few weak characters or down-and-outs, skid-row types. The 'sober' citizen takes comfort in the sight of the stereotype drinker in the town centre or around the railway station. But these drinkers are only the surface evidence of the problem. There are many more whose harmful drinking is unrecognized or goes unremarked. They are often in apparently stable situations.

In fact the social background of problem drinkers closely approximates to that of the ordinary socially integrated citizen (Edwards *et al.* 1967). An analysis of 3000 cases dealt with by the Merseyside, Lancashire and Cheshire Council on Alcoholism over a five-year period revealed 452 individual professions or occupations and no preponderance in any of the five social classes. The same study showed 75 per cent of the people seeking help were still in employment. This proportion was confirmed when the analysis was extended over a longer period of time (Kenyon 1977). If it were more generally appreciated that drink-related problems do not just occur among some special minority group, there would no doubt be a greater recognition of the consequential problems caused at work. As it is, there is still a tendency for senior managers to say "of course, we don't have any problems here". In fact, a study of two Scottish regions and one south-east England region showed that 10 per cent of drinking males had experienced problems at work (Kreitman 1986, Latcham *et al* 1984).

Accidents

One result of these problems is the role of alcohol in accidents. For example, in 1979-80 there were 92 fatal accidents reported to the Health and Safety Executive in Scotland. Blood-alcohol concentrations were estimated in 35 cases. While it should be noted that a blood-alcohol measure was taken in less than 40 per cent of the fatalities, it is surely not without significance that in 20 per cent of these 35 fatalities the blood-alcohol concentration was over the legal driving limit (Beaumont and Allsop 1983).

Further evidence of the relationship between alcohol and accidents was obtained from a large engineering company in 1983. The employment records of all individuals identified and referred as problem drinkers under the company's alcohol policy were examined. Of the 48 employees referred for help over a four-year period, 32 had industrial accidents in the three-year period prior to referral. The company safety manager estimated that this was 50 per cent higher than the workforce average (Beaumont and Allsop 1983).

The same study ascertained that over a two-year period there were 21 known alcohol-related accidents out of a total notified of 101, ie just under 21 per cent. Compared with 61 per cent of non-alcohol-related accidents, 81 per cent of the alcohol-related ones were of three basic types: falls (33 per cent), handling (29 per cent) and 'stepping and striking' (19 per cent). Perhaps more significantly it was revealed that 43 per cent of the alcohol-related accidents occurred between 8am and 10am and 33 per cent between 1pm and 2pm. By contrast, only 19 per cent of non-alcohol-related accidents occurred in the same time periods. Further, it is possible that the proportion recorded as alcohol-related is an under-estimate. This is because the company was inclined to take disciplinary action against employees found to have been drinking before an accident. It is likely, therefore, that workers involved in accidents would be reluctant to admit to alcohol consumption beforehand.

Hangovers

The time clustering of accidents is perhaps associated with hangovers and in some cases the lingering intoxicating effects of the previous night's drinking. In a survey of almost 2000 adults carried out for the DHSS (Wilson 1980) about one in ten fully employed men and one in twenty fully employed women reported feeling the effects of a hangover, while at work or doing housework, during the previous three months. Similar proportions admitted to heavy evening consumption before a working day during the last week.

Among heavy drinkers the proportions were much higher, with 45 per cent of men and 28 per cent of women reporting after-effects in the last week.

There were no consistent differences between manual and non-manual workers, although it was thought the former may have been reluctant to admit to the after-effects of heavy drinking. The survey showed that younger people are more likely to be heavy drinkers than older people and consequently more likely to suffer from hangovers at work. It was also found that heavy drinkers were more likely to drink excessively at lunch time. Heavy drinkers were defined in this study as those men who had consumed more than 50 units of alcohol (eg 25 pints of beer) during the last week and women who had consumed more than 35 units (eg 35 glases of wine) during the same period (Wilson 1980). These definitions are related to the then prevailing conventional wisdom about safe drinking levels. Currently (1988) these heavy drinking definitions would be revised downwards to 35 units for men and 21 units for women. (NB. The sensible level for drinkers to aim for is a weekly limit of no more than 21 units for men and no more than 14 units for women).

Clearance times

It is not just a matter of hangovers. Drinkers do not always appreciate how long it takes for alcohol to leave the body. For the average person it will take one hour for the alcohol in a half pint of beer, a glass of wine or a single measure of spirits to be cleared. Nothing can be done to speed up the process. This is because only 2-5 per cent can be got rid of through the kidneys (urine), lungs (breath) and sweat. The rest has to be burned up by the liver and it can only do so at the rate of one unit per hour.

All this means that after a night's heavy drinking a person's body may still contain enough alcohol next morning to exceed the legal limit for driving and to affect work performance adversely. Drinking three pints of beer (6 units) at lunch time would mean being over the drink driving limit well into the afternoon and could affect work performance for the whole of the afternoon. Any lunch-time drinker topping up on the way home from work should also remember that they could be in excess of the legal limit for driving.

Absence

There are other matters to consider. Employees who drink too much or at inappropriate times will often come late to work in the morning or after lunch. They will want to leave the job more frequently than others and their general efficiency is probably reduced because of a lack of alertness, judgement and accuracy. What might be called sickness presence as opposed to sickness absence.

The latter is a major problem caused by alcohol misuse. There have been several studies of absenteeism, including an early study in an American steel mill. It found that 3 per cent of the male work force lost time because of drinking. On average, each of the 352 workers concerned lost 22 days a year (Stevenson 1942). Twenty-five years later a study of clients attending alcohol information centres in Glasgow, Gloucester and Liverpool discovered that 98 per cent had lost time from work during the previous year. On average the number of days lost was 86 (Edwards *et al,* 1967). It is important to note that alcohol problems will rarely be shown explicitly on medical certificates as a reason for absence.

In a study of sickness certificates covering patients attending an alcohol treatment unit in Manchester only 3 per cent had 'alcoholism' recorded on their certificates (Saad and Madden 1976). This was in spite of the fact that on average in the previous year those in work had lost 70 days from work. Those at that time out of work had lost 208 days.

Among other reasons given were 36 per cent 'psychiatric', 10 per cent 'accidents' and 14 per cent 'respiratory disorders'. There needs always to be an awareness therefore that the real reason for absence may be hidden by the apparent cause given on a sickness certificate. Overall, drinkers take four times as many days off work as other workers (Saad and Madden 1976). It is estimated that 8-14 million days are lost each year as a result of excessive drinking (Holtermann and Burchell 1981). That is two to four times more than the days lost from strikes in a normal year (*Social Trends* 1986).

Who suffers?

These problems militate against the benefits that should accrue from training and experience. They might also lead to misconduct and bad blood between workmates or between management and employees. It is not only the employer who suffers from these adverse effects of drinking. An employee might earn less because of a deterioriation in his or her ability to do the job as quickly or as well as before. Promotion prospects might be marred. Worse, an employee might be injured and suffer short or sometimes long-term physical and mental ill health, perhaps leading to unemployment (Edwards *et al* 1967).

It is not only shop-floor workers who are affected. As was shown earlier, problem drinking pervades the whole of society and therefore will be found at every level in an organization. At whatever level it occurs the consequences could prove costly, but particularly so if someone in a senior position is affected. Apart from a reduced level of efficiency the person concerned may be quite incapable of taking rational decisions at crucial moments in an organization's fortunes. Not only might current business opportunities be lost but future business forgone if, say, a company's reputation suffers because of the behaviour of a senior representative. Further, it is hard to imagine delicate personnel work, negotiations or staff appointments being undertaken well by someone affected by drinking. If eventually such a person has to be dismissed or leaves because of alcohol-induced ill health, the whole process of replacement could be extremely expensive in lost experience and new recruitment.

Occupations at risk

Some specific jobs have been found to carry high risks of heavy and often harmful drinking, including high death rates due to liver cirrhosis (Plant 1987). The following table (page 17) gives one indication of those groups who are particularly vulnerable. It shows 32 occupational groups in Britain which had above-average rates of death from liver cirrhosis between 1979 and 1983.

The table shows a range of high-risk occupations from nurses and nurse administrators who are 8 per cent more likely to die from liver cirrhosis than the average occupied person, to publicans who are more than ten times likely to do so. Identifying the common factors in these varying kinds of occupation and those such as company directors and executives found to be at risk in other studies is not easy. Among the most often suggested are the following:

Liver Cirrhosis Mortality Amongst British Males in Different Occupations (1979-80, 1982-83)

Occupational group	Mortality Rate
Average occupation	100
Publicans	1017
Foremen, ships, lighters and other vessels	900
Deck, engine-room hands, bargemen, lightermen and boatmen	873
Barmen	612
Managers of hotels, clubs etc, and in entertainment and sports	553
Waiters and bar staff	461
Deck, engineering and radio officers and ship pilots	417
Electrical engineers (so described)	387
Hotel and residential club managers	342
Officers (ships and aircraft), air traffic planners and controllers	337
Innkeepers	315
Officers, UK armed forces	303
Catering supervisors	297
Fishermen	296
Bus conductors	277
Chefs, cooks	265
Restaurateurs	263
Authors, writers, journalists	261
General labourers	247
Travel stewards and attendants, hospital and hotel porters	245
Drivers' mates	225
Actors, musicians, entertainers, stage managers	222
Winders, reelers	202
Bakers, flour confectioners	157
Judges, barristers, advocates, solicitors	155
Salesmen, sales assistants, shop assistants, shelf fillers, petrol pump forecourt attendants	147
Other domestic and school helpers	141
Garage proprietors	140
Clergy, ministers of religion	131
Pharmacists, radiographers, therapists	127
Medical and dental practitioners	115
Nurse administrators, nurses	108

SOURCE: OPCS, combined tables from M A Plant, *Drugs in Perspective,* 1987, 92, and Labour Research Department, *Bargaining Report,* December 1986, 11.

1. availability of alcohol at work (eg drinks trade)
2. social pressure to drink at work (eg servicemen, seamen and journalists)
3 separation from normal social or sexual relationships (eg servicemen, seamen, commercial travellers)
4 freedom from supervision (eg doctors, lawyers, executives)
5 very high or low income levels (eg professionals, the unemployed or unskilled workers)
6 strains and stresses, eg danger (servicemen, seamen); responsibility (nurses, doctors, lawyers, executives); lack of job security (actors); boredom (assembly line)
7 recruitment of so-called 'unusual people' predisposed to drinking heavily (eg merchant navy)

(Adapted from Plant 1987)

The costs

There is a dearth of research on which to base confident estimates of the costs of alcohol misuse to industry and the country. Nevertheless, even on the limited epidemiological evidence available it has been conservatively estimated that the total resource costs in England and Wales at 1987 prices is about £2 billion. This figure includes nothing for reduced efficiency but does take account of close on £800 million for sickness absence. It also takes into account £183 million for alcohol-related unemployment (based on McDonnell and Maynard 1985).

The magnitude of these figures is almost certainly an underestimate, as a comparison with similar work in the USA suggests. In 1975 the United States government estimated that the social cost of alcohol misuse was $43 billion. That figure was thought to be unduly cautious and in 1983 a revised estimate of $73 billion was published by economist Leonard Schifrin. He provided a further updated estimate for 1979 of $113 billion (*The Drinking Revolution* 1987). Even without allowing for further updating to present prices, but taking account of the different population sizes, that would be equivalent to a figure for England and Wales of £23.6 billion at April 1988 exchange rates, twelve times McDonnell and Maynard's figure. For the United Kingdom the equivalent figure would be £27 billion.

There are some factors which would lead to an expectation of greater alcohol misuse in the USA. Consumption of alcohol per head is 17 per cent higher than in Britain, medical costs and wages are higher, more people own and drive cars, and the consequences of violent crime are considerably more serious. However, such factors are unlikely to reduce the comparable figures by more than half (*The Drinking Revolution* 1987). The American studies might suggest therefore that the figure for the UK could be as high as £13.5 billion. Either end of the scale, the £2 billion based on British research or the £13.5 billion extrapolated from American figures, makes it clear that there are substantial savings to be made if alcohol misuse can be cut down. A strategy for helping and prevention is needed, especially at the workplace.

Drugs

Chapter 1 looked at the way in which illegal drug use was discussed within our society and showed that the issue was more complex than saying simply drugs are bad, therefore they must not be taken.

Drug users are not as easily or readily definable as might be assumed from the images portrayed in the media. The classic image of a young person suffering from acute acne with an ashen pallor who is usually unemployed is erroneous. An attempt has been made to show that drug users come from a variety of backgrounds which cut across most of the social groupings including class, gender and race. The vast majority of users take drugs recreationally either at weekends or parties or on special occasions and rarely experience problems with their use other than through the law. As such most of us would not be able to recognize who takes drugs and who does not. Recreational users like social drinkers will conduct their lives as any one else would, holding similar values and principles and reflecting the multiplicity of opinions within our society. Those that are of concern are users whose drug use has become more than just pleasure-seeking, or experimentation. In the Introduction a definition was outlined of what problematic drug use is and from this definition it is possible to see how people's lives may be affected. Ultimately it is necessary to look at how this relates to work and whether there is a role at the workplace for assisting people to overcome their problems.

The CBI, in its document *Danger: Drugs at Work* (1986), quotes a figure of 25 per cent of those presenting to agencies with a drugs problem as being in full-time employment. The International Labour Organization's figure for employed drug *users* is 62 per cent. Obviously it is difficult to obtain an accurate figure as research into illegal activities is very difficult to achieve. This is due to the fear those involved with such activities have of being discovered through disclosure. It can be assumed however that there will be people in employment who are experiencing problems with drug use and that this may have an effect on their performance, much in the same way as with alcohol.

So what are the kinds of problems that drugs can pose for the user and subsequently their work? Much will depend on the drug used, the quantity taken and the length of time someone has been using it.

All drugs have the ability to affect people's physical and psychological functioning, particularly if the person's use has become chaotic. Chaotic, in this context, means that there is no stable or controlled use of the drug involved and that the person is using it to cope with problems that they may find otherwise difficult or unbearable. Where this kind of use obtains, those around the user will become aware of changes in mood, ranging from what can be termed as normal functioning through to erratic behaviour, irritability and depression.

For those who are using drugs such as opiates or tranquillizers physical withdrawal symptoms may make others aware of a possible drug problem. With other drugs, such as stimulants, the changes are predominantly psychological as outlined above, although it has been noted that, with sustained use, stimulants can cause audio and visual distortion.

All of these conditions will affect the person's ability to function in their day to day tasks. Work colleagues, by their relationship to the user, may be the first to notice these changes, either because of the quality of the work they have produced or simply because the day to day contact becomes more strained. It is not simply the drug user who is affected. The drug user's colleagues may now be affected by the changes in behaviour of the user. Often families, friends and relatives are also affected where they either suspect or know that someone close to them is using drugs. This can result in the person becoming anxious about possible outcomes of use, which may then affect their performance in work.

In understanding how drugs might become a problem for the user's colleagues or their friends and relatives, it is necessary to recognise that at some point the workplace might also be affected. It is important therefore to examine what role, if any, work can play in the process of enabling someone to overcome their problems.

Some employers, as with alcohol, may prefer to ignore the issue altogether or simply dismiss the person concerned. However, by taking this course of action, there is a risk of exacerbating the problem. For many drug users who lose their work, their use escalates and becomes even more of a problem. This may lead some into illegal activities as a method of obtaining further supplies of their drugs. If this is the case, then perhaps some burden of responsibility could be laid at the door of the employer.

A more constructive way of tackling the issue would be to offer some form of assistance for dealing with drug use. Such an approach would require a policy with clear guidelines and boundaries.

By establishing such a policy the employer will reap benefits much in the same way as we outlined in the section on alcohol. The employer will not lose good workers, or have to go through the lengthy and expensive process of recruitment and training. Similarly, workers will feel more confident in knowing that their employer is not simply using them as a means to enhance profits. but has a genuine care for those it employs. Furthermore, if no policy exists, employers may find themselves involved in time-consuming disputes among workers who are affected by an individual user with no clear structure for dealing with them. All in all it would make for sound business sense to establish such a framework.

Chapter Three
Alcohol and Drugs Policies

Ossie O'Brien and Hugh Dufficy

A systematic approach

It has been shown that most problem drinkers and a small but significant number of drug users are in employment, resulting in more accidents, greater absenteeism and inefficiency, possibly bad decision-making and potentially the loss of highly trained personnel. Enough is known to suggest that these problems should be taken seriously. This might elicit a variety of responses. A company's management could decide to dismiss anyone thought to have a drink or drugs problem. However, this might not be a very wise response especially as it could mean being on the losing end of an unfair dismissal claim. Nevertheless, it is not unknown for an employer to say "yes we have a policy, we sack them".

While most employers would probably reject such a nihilistic view they may not want, or know enough, to adopt a more positive approach. In many cases a blind eye will be turned to the problem, and a form of implicit collusion practised. Yet, if 75 per cent of problem drinkers and 25 per cent of problem drug users are in employment, where better than the workplace to mount a helping and preventive programme? Where better for a policy designed to aid rehabilitation, including a return to a work peformance satisfying to both employer and employee?

It is not just a matter of altruism. There are benefits to be gained in adopting a systematic approach to dealing with alcohol and drug problems at work. For employers, it should show results in economic terms. Fewer accidents, less time off from alcohol and drug-related sickness, better relationships, more co-operation, improved judgement and surer decision-making will all pay dividends in the form of greater quantity and quality of production. Costs can also be saved by avoiding the need to replace expensively recruited and trained staff, especially in key positions.

For employees, there should be greater job satisfaction and increased job security to go with their improved general well-being. In some cases it may mean a liberation of talents that had previously been hidden or inhibited. It could open up prospects for promotion which had previously been denied to employees known to have a drink or drug problem. No doubt also there would be greater respect between colleagues who no longer have to cover up for each other out of misplaced loyalty.

A formal policy

These benefits will not be brought about by chance or good intentions. There needs to be a well-thought-out strategy for reducing alcohol and drug misuse at the workplace and returning employees to an acceptable level of job performance and personal well-being. At the heart of such a strategy should be a formal policy setting out the procedures for helping employees identified as having alcohol or drug-related work problems to achieve these ends. A 1981 Health and Safety Executive report suggested that the objective of an alcohol policy "should be to assist employees who are problem drinkers, in the interests of health and safety at work, by setting out the organization's intentions with regard to confidentiality, job security, sickness benefits, pension rights and disciplinary procedures concerning problem drinking". These sentiments should be extended to include problem drug users.

Any organization taking heed of the Health and Safety Executive's views should have regard to certain principles. An alcohol and drugs policy should not be concerned with an employee's private life but with work performance, conduct and relationships at work. Central to it should be an assurance to all employees that anyone identified as having an alcohol or drug problem would be regarded in the same way as someone with a more generally accepted health problem requiring treatment. As problem drinkers and drug users are known to exist at every level in society, and therefore at every level of work, the policy should apply to everyone regardless of sex, status or seniority.

An alcohol and drugs policy is most likely to be carried out if it is based on wide consultation and, where appropriate, negotiation with trade unions. It should be set out in a formal document for circulation to all employees and might usefully say in a preamble why the policy is thought to be necessary. The known effects on the workplace of excessive or inappropriate drinking or drug use could be stated along with any evidence gathered in the organization concerned. While it is not possible to lay down hard and fast rules for every organization, there are a number of guidelines which might be followed.

The policy could include:

1 an assurance that any employee identified as having an alcohol or drug related problem adversely affecting the work situation will be offered assistance in obtaining advice and whatever other help is considered necessary after an assessment by appropriate people

2 the right to have any absence from work considered necessary for treatment regarded in the same way as any other absence under the sickness provisions of the contract of employment

3 an opportunity to discuss the matter once it has become evident or suspected that work performance is being affected by alcohol or drug-related problems

4 the right to be accompanied at any discussion by a friend or trade union representative

5 the establishment of links with appropriate alcohol or drug agencies to which an employee can be referred for help or

6 a recognition that where an employing organization provides its own treatment or counselling services the staff concerned would be of the same professional standard as available in outside agencies

7 the safeguarding of all benefits and employment rights during any period of treatment

8 a commitment, unless there is a compelling reason otherwise, that when an employee is judged fit to resume work it will be in the original post

9 an offer of suitable alternative employment if it is not possible or is considered inadvisable for the employee to return to the original post, with the right to take up the matter in the grievance procedure if dissatisfied

10 the procedure for assisting an employee with alcohol or drug-related work problems

11 a provision which makes clear that, if an employee refuses the offer of help, the matter may be referred to the disciplinary procedure if the work situation warrants it

12 a provision to refer the matter to the disciplinary procedure if an employee denies the existence of an alcohol or drug-related problem or discontinues a course of treatment and then reverts to an unsatisfactory level of conduct or work performance

13 the possibility of considering on its merits any reversion after treatment to an unsatisfactory level of conduct or work performance caused by alcohol – or drug-related work problems

14 a commitment to confidentiality possibly based on a contract between the employer, the employee and the alcohol or drug helping agency about what can and cannot be disclosed

15 a mechanism for monitoring, evaluating and periodically reviewing the working of the policy on at least a twelve-month basis

16 the designation of management responsibilities for ensuring the policy is carried out

17 an education programme designed to raise the awareness of all staff about the possible harmful consequences of excessive alcohol or drug consumption and the concepts of sensible and safe drinking

18 a training programme to equip specifically designated members of staff with the skills and knowledge necessary to carry out their duties under the policy

Possible objections

There are a number of reasons why employers may not want to respond in this way to alcohol or drug problems in the workplace. Many worry that if they were known to have an alcohol and drug policy they would be perceived as having major problems and their public image would suffer. High profile companies in both manufacturing and service industries seem particularly prone to this view. If these companies do have policies they are often reluctant to publicize the fact. Some companies fear the cost would be too great and are concerned about being required to meet the charges which might be incurred in referring employees to external rehabilitation services. Often they are unaware of the range of external support services available and therefore think that an alcohol and drug policy will require specialist personnel to be employed. Even when companies are aware of the problems and the services available they might still argue that it is a matter for the community as a whole and not employers.

Most of these responses are based on ignorance and/or an unwillingness to think the matter through. Rather than injure the company's public image it is likely to be seen as forward-thinking and concerned for its employees if a policy is adopted. The cost need not be prohibitive as services available in the community are usually free. Private treatment facilities can be expensive but more often than not are unnecessary. However, a company may sometimes want to use them for reasons other than the standard of services available there and elsewhere in the public sector.

Outside help

It is important for companies and other organizations to know what kind of services are available and at what cost. Local alcohol and drug agencies can usually provide a comprehensive counselling service for individuals and in some cases can also cater for families. Where necessary, they can also arrange for a period of hospitalization. Organizations with an occupational health service might themselves provide a counselling service. If they do, it is essential that the staff concerned are trained to the appropriate professional standard. It is a matter for careful thought. Should an employee require treatment beyond counselling it would be rare, except perhaps in a health authority, for the answer to be found in-house. Even with counselling, the best course would normally be to link up with an outside agency.

Outside agencies may also be looked to for the provision of the education and training programme essential to any serious alcohol and drugs policy. They can advise on the design and printing of posters, leaflets and maybe a booklet aimed at raising the awareness of all employees. Expert trainers can be provided by them to train members of staff with special responsibilities within the policy. There will be costs involved but those organizations known to have carried out training programmes have seen these costs as an integral part of their training budgets. Once the decision to have an alcohol and drugs policy is taken it should be accepted that education and training are central to its success.

Cost-effective?

The actual cost of instituting a policy and an educational and training programme will obviously vary with the organization. One major service sector company is known to have budgeted for £20,000 in the first year. However, it claims the policy will pay for itself if only two employees are rehabilitated each year (Private Conference Paper 1988). A big public corporation is said to have spent £100,000 in developing a comprehensive health promotion policy which includes alcohol and drug problems. This sum included staff costs, and a twenty-minute video, a training presenter's brief and a health road-show to take round all its employees. But even in this case the operation is now said to be 'in profit'. The video and training presenter's brief sold enough copies in little more than a year to break even. It is also claimed that productivity has improved through guidance on sensible drinking, early intervention and improvements in staff morale. The important consideration is to ensure that an alcohol and drugs policy has a budget commensurate to its aims.

The cost of not having a policy is put in stark perspective by a senior manager in a UK high-tech company. He has said that the 20 worst drinkers in his organization cost the company £½ million a year (private communication). On the other hand the reported results of having a policy can be quite spectacular. A study of the first year's effect of an alcohol and drugs programme in a large car-manufacturing company showed there had been:

50 per cent reduction in occupational injuries

60 per cent reduction in sickness and accident benefit claims

80 per cent reduction in absenteeism

40 per cent reduction in lost time
50 per cent reduction in grievance and disciplinary action
(International Labour Organization 1987)

Overall, the message is that policies are likely to be cost-effective and companies should develop them in their own interest.

How many policies now?

Just how many organizations have adopted alcohol and or drug policies of this kind is difficult to say. The national agency on alcohol misuse, Alcohol Concern, has a library of just over one hundred written alcohol policies but, except for 24 from brewery companies, they were not collected in a systematic way. It is not possible, therefore, to know what they represent in terms of the proportions likely to have policies in the sectors from which they are drawn. The 24 brewery company policies were gathered in response to a letter sent to all brewery companies which in 1986 numbered 68 (Brewers' Society, 1986). So we know that at least 35 per cent of companies in this line of production have policies. Almost certainly that is well above the proportion for employing organizations generally.

In 1986 the Labour Research Department conducted a survey to assess the impact of the joint publication of *The Problem Drinker at Work* by the Health and Safety Executive and the Department of Employment. This publication had recommended that management should, in consultation with any recognized trade unions, agree and implement a statement of policy towards the problem drinker at work. (We would say that a drugs policy should also be incorporated into this.)

Only 44 replies were received to 400 questionnaires, an 11 per cent response rate. Of these 12 (27 per cent) had a written or formal policy, three (7 per cent) said they were in the process of negotiating a policy and 22 (50 per cent) had no policy and no intention of introducing one (Labour Research Department, 1986).

It is impossible to draw firm conclusions from such a small sample of companies but it is perhaps not unreasonable to assume that the majority of the 356 companies who failed to reply did not have policies. That would be borne out by the experience of alcohol agencies working in this field. An informed guess might be that no more than 20 per cent of companies have formal alcohol policies. Even less will have a drugs policy. The proportion among public authorities will be higher and is already growing. An increasing number of local government authorities are developing policies and an added impetus will be given to similar developments in health authorities as a result of the publication of national guidelines (HEA 1988). However, research is needed to establish the scope for overall development in all these spheres.

Chapter Four

Implementing an Alcohol and Drugs Policy

Ossie O'Brien and Hugh Dufficy

Preparatory steps

The idea of having an alcohol and drugs policy may be initiated by either external or internal sources. Whatever the source, there needs to be a recognition that setting up and implementing the policy can be a lengthy process. However, the time can be minimized by drawing on the experience of others. This experience shows that the following preparatory steps are necessary:

1 establishing the need for a policy
2 consulting key personnel
3 setting detailed policy-making in motion
4 determining aims and objectives
5 drafting policy and carrying out further consultations

Establishing the need

Not everyone in an organization will be convinced of the need for an alcohol and drugs policy. Some employees, including managers, may be positively frightened by such a development because it will face them with their own behaviour and their attitudes towards that of others. It is essential, therefore, to seek maximum commitment. This will most likely be achieved if a clear case is made for a policy, the potential benefits demonstrated and employees reassured about its helping nature and intentions. To do this effectively the person (probably the personnel manager) given the job of progressing the policy should use the information in this book to become familiar with the case for an alcohol and drugs policy. The information can then become the basis for convincing others involved in the process. Ideally, it should be localized for more immediate impact by conversion into the circumstances of the organization concerned. This will mean looking in a new light at the organization's own statistics relating to accidents, absenteeism, lateness, discipline, sickness, work performance and mortality.

In preparation for a later evaluation of the policy information could also be collected on employees' knowledge of and attitudes towards alcohol and drugs. Information on the consumption of alcohol might also be gathered but it is unlikely that anyone will own up to using illegal drugs.

Consulting key personnel

Once the case for an alcohol and drugs policy has been assembled it should be discussed with those people who will be crucial to its success. This includes the board of directors (or its equivalent in a public authority) without whose commitment a policy is unlikely ever to get off the ground. Not only will the board have to sanction the principle but also agree the resources needed to carry it out. The personnel director (or equivalent) would normally be the appropriate advocate at this level though it may sometimes be advisable to bring in someone from an outside alcohol and drugs agency to make a presentation.

If the board gives the go ahead, the personnel director may want to be involved in the detailed preparation of the policy, but more usually it will be the personnel manager who will see it through from this stage. The precise people to be consulted will vary from place to place but they should include anyone who is likely to be involved in the preparation, implementation and evaluation of the policy. It is important, too, to remember those individuals and groups whose influence needs to be recognized and engaged. The following list is not necessarily exhaustive but indicates who should not be excluded:

senior managers
departmental managers
supervisors
occupational health staff
personnel officers and trainers
health and safety representatives
shop stewards and staff representatives

Perhaps the best way of consulting these interested members of staff would be through a joint discussion of the reasons for the policy proposal and the principles on which it would be based.

Some benefit may be gained if the discussion is informed by the involvement of a representative of an external alcohol and drugs agency.

Working out the policy

Following the initial consultation, thought will need to be given to the most appropriate way of working out the details of the policy. In some organizations the personnel manager will simply be expected to get on with the production of the policy. However, in others, especially bigger organizations or public authorities, the most effective way will be to set up a working party drawn from the individuals and representative groups consulted. Anyone who can offer specific help or expertise should be included. Expert advice from outside might also be usefully employed.

The job of the working party will be to prepare the policy and to work out the procedure through which it will be implemented. It will have to establish the financial and staffing commitments required for the effective application of the policy and the availability of the resources to match them. Members of the working party could also be the communication links with the constituencies from which they are drawn. In effect they will be the agents through which commitment to the policy is obtained.

Aims and objectives

The first task of the working party will be to determine the aims and objectives of the policy. These might vary according to the way the problems being dealt with are perceived. However, there are a number of general aims which should apply everywhere. For example, a prime aim should be to provide a safe and healthy working environment. Within this general aim should be the desire to contribute to the health and well being of employees through the promotion of safe and sensible drinking habits and a knowledge of alcohol and drugs which will prevent their misuse. Another related aim might be to work towards an organizational climate in which employees are actively discouraged from drinking during working hours and are made aware of the possible harmful consequences of drinking or drug taking before going to work. Where employees are already known to be consuming alcohol or using drugs in ways which lead to problems at work the aim of the policy should be to encourage them to seek help, usually by referral to an appropriate agency for diagnosis and subsequent counselling or other treatment. Related to this is the essential aim of ensuring that all key staff are trained to recognize when alcohol and drug misuse are contributing to poor work performance. The overall objective of the policy must be a healthy workforce as free as possible from alcohol or drug misuse, working to a satisfactory level of efficiency.

Drafting the policy

Once the aims and objectives of the policy are determined the working party can concentrate on settling the details. In doing so it should be guided by the principles laid down in chapter 3. The procedure for implementing the policy should be spelt out and the roles of everyone involved made clear. There should be a specific commitment to an education and training programme and a procedure agreed for monitoring and evaluating the impact of the policy.

It should not be seen as a policy for dealing only with 'alcoholics' or 'drug addicts'. Very few employees, if any, would identify themselves with such concepts. The policy should make clear that its intention is to help employees who have been identified as having alcohol and drug-related work problems. But it should also make clear that it is concerned with the impact on work of inappropriate consumption of alcohol, eg at lunch-time or before coming on to a night shift. Indeed the policy should mainly be about establishing good practice in the behaviour of the individual employee and in the organizational context within which the employee works.

Once the working party has agreed a draft of the policy it would be beneficial if there were to be a further process of consultation. The policy will no doubt have to go back to the board for approval but the consultation should include everyone who will be involved in its implementation. Where employees are organized in trade unions, their representatives will rightly expect to be consulted. In some cases both management and trade unions may want the policy to be a jointly agreed one. In these circumstances the consultation may in effect become more akin to negotiation. Either way the policy should benefit from critical scrutiny and thereby become more acceptable. Whoever is involved in this final stage of consultation and whatever the procedure, it would be wise to set a time limit otherwise a long time can elapse before the policy is completed.

The timescale must be realistic if the consultation is to be genuine and commitment to the policy gained. Equally, care should be taken not to set unrealistic aims and objectives and to make sure that adequate resources are available to carry through the policy successfully. The working party should check that the alcohol and drugs policy does not contradict other policies and that it is clearly seen as an alternative to the disciplinary procedure.

Implementing the policy

It is not unknown for an organization to think that once it has its policy down on paper that is the end of the matter. A formal statement is important but there must also be a structure for its implementation. There must be people at different levels in the organization with responsibility for carrying out the policy. If they are to do so effectively their roles will need to be defined. These roles may vary according to the organization but the following guidelines might be borne in mind.

Role of management

It is essential that managers are fully familiar with the procedures and content of the policy. They have a responsibility to ensure that employees understand what is expected of them under it, and need to be alert to and monitor changes in work performance, attendance, sickness and accident patterns. When employees are showing signs of possible alcohol or drug misuse managers should be able to recognize them and have the confidence to intervene at an early stage. In dealing with problem situations they should be able to identify any aspects of the work which could also be contributing to alcohol or drug misuse and, where possible, change them. Overall, managers should set a good example through a responsible use of alcohol and by not using drugs. At the same time they should try to avoid value judgements about the alcohol or drug habits of their employees.

Role of occupational health staff

Occupational health staff will be expected to provide guidance and advice, sometimes directly and sometimes through management, to employees who have behaviour or work-performance problems which might be related to alcohol or drug misuse. Once a policy is underway and accepted, occupational health staff may find they have to provide assessments for employees voluntarily seeking help. More usually, however, they will be responding to referrals from personnel or line managers. Either way, their role will be to provide an impartial, confidential service to employees which in some organizations may include counselling. More often, after assessment, they will be responsible for referring employees to other agencies. They will also have an important part to play in promoting knowledge of alcohol and drugs and in encouraging sensible drinking and the avoidance of drugs.

Role of personnel management

The personnel director should have overall responsibility for ensuring the alcohol and drugs policy is implemented and that it includes a training dimension. Day to day responsibility for running and co-ordinating the policy should rest with the personnel manager. Depending on the size and management structure of the organization it could be the personnel manager or personnel officers who have responsibility for referring employees for assistance. They will need to be trained in appropriate interviewing and basic counselling skills. As with line managers they will not be expected to make expert diagnoses but should be equipped to make a judgement about the need for referral either to the occupational health service or an outside agency. Alternatively, depending on the case, they may have to advise on the appropriateness of the disciplinary procedure. It is the personnel department's responsibility to ensure that statistics are kept in such a way that they will facilitate the effectiveness of the policy. Personnel managers and officers will also in many cases be involved in planning and taking part in training courses.

Role of training officers

Training is the *sine qua non* of an alcohol and drugs policy. It is for the training officers to plan and provide it, perhaps in conjunction with an external agency. Their task is to devise methods, materials and curricula which will complement the policy by raising general awareness of alcohol and drug-related work problems and provide the skills essential for dealing with them and the employees directly concerned.

Role of trade union representatives
Where employees are organized in trade unions their representatives will have a part to play in consultations, and maybe negotiations, about the content and implementation of the alcohol and drugs policy. These representatives could play a key role in informing their members about the policy and encouraging them to take part in appropriate education and training programmes. They could help to instil sufficient confidence in the policy so that any of their members in need of help might seek it voluntarily. Where union members become officially caught up in the policy their representatives will want to advise them of their rights and responsibilities. If requested, they will also usually have the right to represent them in any problem or dispute about the application of the policy. Finally, they could be important figures in the rehabilitation of any union member who has been helped through the alcohol and drugs policy and received treatment of some kind.

Role of employees
Once the development of an alcohol and drugs policy is underway, there is some responsibility on employees to find out about alcohol and drugs and their possible effect on work and health. If they are to benefit from the policy or, conversely, not fall foul of it, they must be familiar with it and its procedures. They should not use alcohol irresponsibly in relation to work and not use illegal drugs. If they are worried about their own drinking or drug taking they should seek help, either within the policy procedures or by self-referral to an outside agency. Equally, they should not collude in covering up for colleagues known to have work problems arising from alcohol or drug misuse. It would be far better for everyone concerned if colleagues known to have alcohol or drug-related problems were encouraged to seek help through the policy.

Limits of responsibility

These guidelines place considerable responsibility on managers and other employees who in most cases will be coming to matters concerning alcohol and drugs for the first time. Too much should not be expected of those with first assessment responsibilities. For example, personnel or line managers who may be responsible for interviewing an employee thought to be experiencing alcohol and drug problems should not be expected to make a diagnosis or an assessment of the treatment needed. Their task would simply be to establish that there is a problem which needs further investigation. Even occupational health service staff will probably require training before being able to go beyond the minimum intervention. Where an organization decides to provide a counselling service for its employees, care should be taken in the recruitment and training of the counsellors. It is important that they should be of an equal standard to counsellors employed by specialist external agencies. Whether there is an internal service of this kind or not, it would be wise to establish a good working relationship with an external alcohol and drugs agency. For the foreseeable future the prevailing practice is likely to be that external agencies will be called upon for counselling and other treatment services. Organizations can be put in touch with appropriate agencies by contacting one of the national bodies listed in Appendix 6.

Education and training

An alcohol and drugs policy without an education and training progamme is meaningless. If the policy is to be taken seriously and have any chance of success there must be an understanding among all employees of what it is trying to do. There must also be specific training for those key people who will be crucial to the effective implementation of the policy. The education and training progamme should not be seen simply as an adjunct to getting the policy underway, but as an integral and continuing part of it. It should be based on defined needs, set aims and objectives, and adequate resources.

The understanding necessary among all employees can be achieved through a general education programme. It should be designed to raise awareness about the nature of alcohol and drugs and the possible harmful consequences if they are misused. Such a programme should also encourage safe and sensible drinking practices and stress the desirability of avoiding all illegal drugs. There should also be an emphasis on the confidential help available to any employee who has alcohol or drug-related problems.

This general education programme will require carefully thought-out means of communication if it is to be effective. Where there are well-established channels of communication they should be used, but, if necessary, new channels should be devised. The methods of communication should be attractive and professionally designed to make an immediate impact. They could include a poster campaign, leaflets with pithy messages and a booklet for every employee describing the policy and good practices in relation to alcohol and drugs. If sufficient resources are available a video might be made for general education and training purposes. When an alcohol and drugs policy is established information about it should become an integral part of induction training for every new employee.

Staff responsible for implementing the policy will have immediate training needs. Once these needs are identified, a systematic training programme should be drawn up which, as appropriate, develops the necessary knowledge and skills. There will be a common core of information and knowledge which everyone will need but other parts of the training programme will vary according to responsibilities. A decision will have to be made as to whether the training programme is to be conducted by internal trainers or specialist trainers imported from an alcohol and drugs agency.

Where an organization has a professional training team it may want the necessry training to be kept in its hands. It will be surprising, however, if the trainers themselves don't need training before shouldering the responsibility. This can be done by an external agency who can equip the trainers to carry the training down through the management and staff structure. Personnel and occupational health staff might also usefully be included in training the trainers. The aim should be to develop a team which can carry training forward on a continuing basis when external support has been withdrawn.

Trainers and potential trainers will require tuition in facts about alcohol and drugs as well as training techniques. For both trainers and line managers, on whom a lot of responsibility will fall, training should seek to develop:

1 a basic factual knowledge of alcohol and drugs and the possible harm that can follow misuse

2 an understanding of the concepts of standard units of drinks, safe limits and sensible drinking

3 an appreciation of the nature and extent of alcohol and drugs problems at the workplace, especially in their own organization

4 a recognition of any special factors present at their own workplace

5 a sound knowledge of the organization's alcohol and drugs policy and procedure and their relationship to disciplinary procedures

6 an awareness of the expectations of the law

7 an ability to identify the signs which might indicate that an employee has an alcohol or drugs problem

8 a capacity for judgeing appropriate ways of dealing with the work problem caused by employees thought to have alcohol or drugs problems

9 a knowledge of the services available for helping employees with alcohol and drugs problems, their referral procedures and methods of treatment

10 an exploration of personal attitudes towards drinking and drug taking and how these might affect the implementation of the policy

11 interviewing and basic counselling skills.

Not everyone involved in the implementation of policy will necessarily need to cover all these areas in their training. However, there are advantages to be gained from having managers, supervisors, personnel officers, occupational health staff, health and safety representatives and trade union representatives together in the same training course. It can result in an appreciation of each other's views and a common approach to the policy. Where training together is not desired decisions will have to be taken about what is relevant to particular responsibilities. One reason which may be considered a good one for not having integrated training is that it can then be built into the existing training programmes of each of the groups concerned. Once a training programme is underway the needs of individuals thereafter, at least as far as management is concerned, can be picked up through performance review interviews where they are in operation.

Developing good practice

The process of adopting a policy and developing an education and training programme soon leads to questions being asked about general practices relating to alcohol and drugs. Thought needs to be given, therefore, to what constitutes good practice. It is not possible to lay down hard and fast rules for every organization, especially as they will be starting from different points of development. For example, in some there may be a long history of strict rules about drinking during working hours while in others the very opposite may be the case. Where there is a tradition of drinking, maybe in a company club, it would be very difficult to move in one fell swoop to a completely 'dry' policy. Any attempt to do so would probably kill the policy before it got off the ground. Nevertheless, these traditions can and should be challenged with the aim of creating an alcohol-free working environment. It would be preferable for such an aim to be achieved voluntarily but there are some workplaces where the imposition of a ban on alcohol at work might reasonably be considered. Hospitals come readily to mind.

In seeking to establish good practice policy makers might fruitfully ask the following questions:

Do personnel or health and safety staff regularly analyse the timing, frequency and location of accidents? Are they competent to identify alcohol or drug-related signs?

Are appropriate staff equipped to identify problem drinkers and drug takers?

What is the organization's attitude towards drug taking or drinking habits, either at interviews or in references?

Are soft, low- and no-alcohol drinks always available at lunchtime and at social functions?

What are the rules about drinking during working hours or immediately before work, especially for those whose jobs make them particularly vulnerable, eg drivers?

Does business always get conducted over liquid lunches – need it do so?

Are rules about alcohol and drug taking consistent throughout the organization?

Is a lack of good facilities at work encouraging employees to go out to licensed premises at lunchtime?

Are workplace rules absolutely clear about bringing alcohol into work, about drinking or drug taking at work, and about what happens if someone is drunk or under the influence of drugs at work?

(Based on Tether and Robinson 1985)

In pursuing these questions there should be no suggestion of a witch-hunt or a big brother approach, otherwise trust in the policy will be destroyed. Nevertheless, asking them is an essential part of laying the groundwork for a successful policy. The answers could help create the right kind of context and atmosphere in which good practice will flourish. Periodic reviews will establish whether good practices are developing and whether further efforts are required to bring about desirable changes.

Monitoring and evaluation

Such reviews, along with an evaluation at specified intervals, should be an integral part of a developing alcohol and drugs policy. They can be done effectively only if the policy is monitored as it goes along, probably by the original working party. If it is not already current practice, comprehensive statistical records should be kept on accidents, sickness, absenteeism, lateness, early retirements because of ill-health and deaths of employees. They should be collated and analysed with the policy in mind. Monitoring also requires keeping records of employees identified as having alcohol or drug problems, how the cases were dealt with, whether the individuals were referred to external agencies, if they co-operated and whether they were successfully rehabilitated personally and as satisfactory employees.

These records will in part provide the basis for evaluating the policy. The evaluation itself should be based on objectives previously set for each stage of the policy's development; say, at the end of the preparatory period and thereafter at twelve-month intervals. These objectives could include targets for a reduction in lateness, disputes, accidents, sickness, absence and frequent absences from the job during working hours. Less tangible phenomena such as improved morale and better co-operation between employees and with management are more difficult to measure but should not be ignored.

There is always the possibility that the whole process of evaluation will be forgotten. The manager or director with overall responsibility for the policy should insist on at least a yearly report of its progress. Any necessary changes arising from an evaluation could then be initiated at the highest level. It would be surprising if the need for changes did not periodically come to light. No policy of any kind is ever perfect.

Perhaps the success or otherwise of a policy might best be evaluated by outsiders. While monitoring might be conducted by an internal working party it is worth considering a comprehensive assessment by outside evaluators, say, on a three-or five-yearly basis. Either way, in evaluating the achievement of objectives, possible weaknesses in the monitoring process need to be taken into account. These might include: choosing a base date against which to measure changes, the difficulty in some jobs of measuring improvements in work performance, the reliability of the statistics, and the possibility that increased awareness brought about by the existence of an alcohol and drugs policy may lead some employees to seek help independently but not want the fact recorded. The main value of outside evaluations should be their objectivity.

It is important that evaluations are planned from the beginning and related to agreed objectives. If the methods used for achieving the objectives are consistent with the policy and any possible monitoring weaknesses recognized, the results should be helpful in assessing the quantitative and qualitative impact of the policy. They should be helpful too in improving the policy and increasing the relevance of the education and training programme to employees generally and key personnel in particular. Finally, evaluation findings can provide the base from which to advance steadily towards the goal of eliminating alcohol and drug misuse at work.

Chapter Five

The Law and Alcohol and Drugs in the Workplace

Alan Bensted

Introduction

The purposes of this chapter are threefold: first to highlight those aspects of the law which most affect the employer when dealing with alcohol and drug-related problems in the workforce; secondly, to establish the pattern of response required of the employer by law; and thirdly, to suggest courses of conduct which ought to be considered, including the introduction of suitable policies (*The Problem Drinker at Work* 1981).

Concern about the role of alcohol in causing accidents at work is reflected in law in the imposition of obligations on the employer to ensure a safe system of work, both under statute as part of the criminal law, such as the Health and Safety at Work Act 1974, and at common law, for example in negligence claims as part of the civil law. Furthermore, in carrying out steps to fulfil this obligation, the employer must pursue a policy which secures a safe environment and which takes account of employment protection rights enjoyed by the employee in question. It is in this latter area that the employer will, for all practical purposes, be called upon to establish a sound policy on alcohol in the workplace, and it is to this that we now turn.

Statutory employment protection

When discussing the employer's response to a worker with an alcohol-related problem, we may be concerned with whether the employer should terminate that individual's employment. Under common law, this is usually straightforward in that full contractual notice may be given to terminate and that is the end of the matter.

Only if full notice was not given would a potential claim for wrongful dismissal arise, and the employer be called upon to justify the summary dismissal. Justification would normally be on the basis of a failure to be ready and willing for work, or a failure to use reasonable skill and care at work, or a failure to obey lawful orders. Only if the employer could not show suitable justification for the summary action would the employee succeed in an action for wrongful dismissal and be entitled to compensation – usually a sum equivalent to the unpaid notice – but not to reinstatement!

By statute law, that is, the Employment Protection Consolidation Act 1978, the employer must always justify dismissal by reference to one of five fair reasons within S.57(1) and (2), no matter whether full notice is, given or not. Having done this, it will be for an industrial tribunal to determine on the facts of the case and, in those circumstances, whether the employer had acted reasonably. In other words, the employer has two hurdles to clear; one is to show a fair reason, the other is to demonstrate that he has acted fairly and reasonably.

Drinking which affects an employee's performance or behaviour in the workplace may fall either under *incapability* or *conduct*. As a capability problem, it is viewed in the form of physical incapacity, or deterioration in competence or personality. From the viewpoint of conduct, it is seen as abusive, disobedient or violent behavior, either on or off duty, frequent lateness or being absent without leave. It is the employer who decides in which of these ways to treat an alcohol problem. Then it is for the industrial tribunal to consider his approach and to determine whether dismissal was a fair and reasonable response to the problem.

But how does the employer decide? In brief, if the employee's misconduct or deteriorating capacity is due to chronic alcoholism, then disciplinary procedure would be considered inappropriate, and sickness procedures should be used instead. The medical background of the employee should be investigated and he should be consulted with, and given time off for treatment. Thus the problem is seen as one of incapability, and treated accordingly.

On the other hand, if chronic alcoholism is not in question, but there occurs a breach of 'no-drinking' or safety rules, then this is a matter of conduct and hence is subject to disciplinary procedures.

The problem, of course, is for the employer to decide early enough which of the two courses to follow to ensure the right reasonable steps are taken in the circumstances. This difficulty is shown in *Strathclyde Regional Council v Syme (1979) EAT 233/79.* Syme had ten years' service as a school janitor. Two years of complaints of heavy drinking led to a disciplinary interview. He had hospital treatment for alcoholism but was discovered drunk again, and dismissed. This was held as unfair dismissal because it was not fair and reasonable; the employer should have seen it as a medical problem and allowed appropriate treatment. 'Capability' would have been an acceptable reason, given Syme's responsibilities to staff and pupils, but the case had been treated as misconduct without consideration for the employee's medical condition.

Some general points on how tribunals view employer treatment and procedures may be given:

1 fairness is always judged by how a reasonable employer would behave under particular circumstances, ie the criteria are objective
2 a reasonable employer may have a range of reasonable responses, from dismissal to transfer or demotion, and these may vary from one employer to another. As long as the employer has pursued *one* of these responses, then it will be a fair dismissal (*British Leyland v Swift* (1981))
3 fairness is judged by the facts known to the employer at the time of dismissal. Subsequent discovery will not affect the substantive issue of dismissal, though it may affect compensation (*Davis v Atkins* (1977))
4 fairness may be judged by reference to relevant Codes of Practice issued by the Department of Employment
5 a failure to follow a disciplinary/dimissal procedure will probably make a dismissal unfair (*Polkey v A E Dayton Services HL* (1987))
6 offenders in the same situation should, as a general rule, not be treated differently (*Post Office v Pennell* (1981))
7 employers should publish clear rules about misconduct or incapability involving alcohol where a breach of those rules could lead to summary dismissal or further procedures. Non-adherence to these rules, however, will not necessarily make a dismissal automatically unfair.

Specific provisions on drinking as a capability problem

Alcohol misuse will often become evident through an employee's deteriorating work performance. The employer should then investigate the causes of this, evaluate the likelihood of improvement and take reasonable measures to bring the employee back to competence. If the employee is discovered to be an alcoholic, then the employer is expected as part of the conduct of good industrial relations to treat this as illness. That is, he must investigate the problem thoroughly, consult with the employee about steps to be taken and encourage him to seek appropriate medical advice (*Spencer v Paragon Wallpapers* (1977)), perhaps through the company doctor, and also allow the employee time off with pay to follow the medical advice given.

Of course, a major problem is the balancing of the employer's needs against the time required for an employee to recover; in short, how long to wait before dismissing the individual. The factors to be considered are these (*British Home Stores v Burchell* (1978)).

1 the nature of the illness: for example, is it diagnosed as acute alcoholism?
2 the likely length of the absence
3 the importance of the employee's position in the organization, and the need to get his work done
4 the ease with which a temporary replacement can be appointed
5 the willingness of the employee to take advice and to undergo treatment.

To summarize, a high degree of employer patience and consideration is required, particularly if the organization is large. A typical approach of tribunals to the above factors may be seen in the case of *Kirkwall Port Employer's Association v Louttit (1982) EAT 52/82.* Louttit was persistently absent through sickness. His employer obtained a medical report which concluded that Louttit had an alcohol problem which made him unfit for work as a docker, and that he needed 6-12 months' treatment to recover. No opportunity was given to Louttit to discuss the report, his own doctor's more hopeful prognosis was not considered and he was not told that his job was in jeopardy. Moreover, he was working competently just prior to dismissal. His employer removed Louttit from the register of dockers and dismissd him with a lump-sum notice compensation. This was held an unfair dismissal. The employer should have considered the nature of Louttit's illness, and consulted with him as to his willingness to undergo treatment.

Opportunities, through consultation, should be allowed to the employee to challenge reports made on him, otherwise there is a risk of unfair dismissal, as in the case of *Dodd v City of Birmingham District Council (1980) COIT 992/235.* Here, an employee of long standing was dismissed without interview on the report of the employer's own doctor. The dismissal was held to be unfair as the medical report was considered insufficient evidence for the dismissal of a long-service employee. The employers should have made further enquiries and given Dodd the opportunity to challenge the medical report.

Once the employer has exhausted all reasonable avenues of assistance to an employee who is either an alcoholic or whose persistent drinking has made him incapable of doing his job properly, then the employee may be fairly dismissed for lack of capability or qualifications. The employer must have a reasonable, honestly held belief that the employee was incapable, have carried out reasonable investigations to substantiate this belief and have exhausted reasonable alternatives to dismissal (*British Home Stores v Burchell* (1978)). Thus in *Carter v Playshire Ltd (1981) COIT 1190/108,* the employer showed tolerance and sympathy to his employee, suggested Alcoholics Anonymous and psychiatric help on the advice of his own doctor; but, when these suggestions were refused, made it clear that dismissal would follow if there was no improvement of conduct. Carter's dismissal was held to be fair, as the employer had exhausted all reasonable courses of action and, given Carter's position as painter/supervisor, could not afford further disruption to take place.

Sometimes an alcohol problem will lead to the loss of a driving licence. The employer here has two alternative reasons for fair dismissal. The first would be under S.57(2)(d) of the Employment Protection Consolidation Act under which an employee could not continue to work in that position (for example, as a driver) without contravening a statutory duty or restriction (that is, the Road Traffic Act). The second fair reason for dismissal would be under S.57(2)(a), that his capability was impaired by his disqualification.

However, the employer must always consider alternatives to dismissal, such as whether a temporary transfer could be made, or the position rendered tenable by the use of public transport or a chauffeur. Essentially, the employer will consider the cost of such measures balanced against factors like the length of service or the importance to the organization of the employee. In *Ashton Paper Mills v Haines (1979) EAT 361/79,* Haines needed to visit various sites as a foreman but was disqualified for one year. There were no alternative positions and no other employee could be spared to drive him. His dismissal was held to be unfair, however, because the employer had not considered whether Haines' offer to employ a driver himself was a reasonable one before dismissing him. This should be compared with the decision in *Roberts v Toyota (GB) Ltd (1980)* where it was held to be fair to dismiss an area sales manager who had been disqualified, despite the willingness of his wife to drive him, because it damaged the company's image to have an 'ambassador' disqualified.

The policy which ought to be adopted towards the problem drinker may be gathered from case decisions, from the Health and Safety Executive guidelines and the draft revised code on disciplinary procedures. This may be summarized as follows:

1 the employer should keep a watchful eye for early signs of drink problems, such as higher levels of absenteeism, inefficient performance, personality changes, irritability, slurred speech, poor timekeeping, impaired memory, anxiety, depression or a decline in personal hygiene
2 the employer should educate the workforce to recognize these symptoms in colleagues, subordinates or themselves and encourage those affected to seek advice
3 medical help should be made available (not necessarily involving only the company doctor) and sick leave or regular treatment sessions should be considered
4 encouragement to pursue such treatment should be given by the employer through consultation
5 all information from such consultations should be treated as confidential
6 the employer should see alcoholism, if being treated under this type of policy, as a mitigating factor in any further disciplinary proceedings

7 relapses should be treated sympathetically. However, although refusing treatment should not (according to the HSE) be a disciplinary offence in itself, a refusal could be met with future disciplinary action for lateness, absence or other offences
8 the employer could consider transfer to less responsible work, though this could mean a down-grading in pay or status. This implies a claim of constructive dismissal by the employee, though it is likely to be a fair dismissal if the employer is acting reasonably and has exhausted other options. The case of *Spiers v Department of Employment* (1982) SCOIT S/778/82 demonstrates this, in which the manager of an Unemployment Benefit Office was held not to have been constructively dismissed despite down-grading because the Department of Employment had repeatedly encouraged him to rehabilitate himself and had given him extended periods of time in which to do so.

Specific provisions on drinking as a conduct problem

In much the same way as other disciplinary offences, drunken behaviour, abusiveness, fighting, unauthorized absence, frequent lateness, drinking during working hours or being inebriated while on duty, are grounds for eventual dismissal for conduct. Similar requirements of investigation, fair procedure and alternative disciplinary measures should be pursued by the employer as, in general, he would with incapability. Avoidance of over-reaction to a minor incident is called for, together with a careful consideration of a summary dismissal for a gross act of misconduct. In general, where the employee is not an alcoholic, employers may take the view that drinking, or being drunk, at work is gross misconduct entailing summary dismissal, provided that the employer has acted fairly and reasonably in the circumstances.

What is important for a fair dismissal is that the following six points are generally adhered to:

1 there should be clear disciplinary rules, warning the employee of the consequences of drunkenness, for example the *Code of Practice on Disciplinary Procedures* 1986 para 7, and these rules should be communicated clearly to the workforce

2 such rules, wherever possible, should be agreed between employer and trade union, and enshrined in a collective agreement

3 drinking offences should clearly figure in the rules, especially those for whose breach there is to be an exceptional response, such as dismissal for the first offence, and such a rule should be incorporated into the employment contract of the individual worker (*Beverstock v Dairy Product Packers* (1981))

4 the employee should be interviewed, not when the offence occurs, but when he is sober, allowing him to deny, give reasons for, or mitigate his offence, or to apologize for it. Summary dismissal must thus be postponed, or an unfair dismissal may occur. In *Charles Letts & Co v Howard* (1976) IRLR 248, Howard was abusive to his manager while drunk, but there had been tension previously between the two. His summary dismissal was held to be unfair because he should have been given the opportunity to put his case and to apologize when sober. Such a decision is likely in cases involving a sudden explosion or loss of temper, as matters could have been put right before it was too late

5 consideration should then be given as to whether a reasonable investigation has been carried out into the case. This does not have to be exhaustive; the employee should usually be interviewed, but not every last witness. For example, in *Gray Dunn v Edwards* (1980) IRLR 23, Edwards was dismissed for drinking before coming on shift, an offence which could lead to summary dismissal. Three senior employees concluded that he was drunk and Edwards admitted his pre-shift drinking. The employer did not hear several witnesses who claimed that he was still capable of doing his job, but the dismissal was considered fair in that there had been an adequate investigation, bearing Edwards' admission in mind

6 finally, the dismissal must be considered as one of a range of sanctions. The punishment must fit the crime, and employers must not consider that all incidents of drinking should automatically lead to dismissal.

Some specific incidents of misconduct leading to dismissal are included as follows:

Where a person is a danger to others

The tribunals take a very strict view where potential danger is involved, so that persons operating machinery or vehicles, or supervising dangerous processes may be fairly dismissed for isolated incidents which do not cause actual injury. The dismissal of a bus driver for drinking one pint of beer during a one-hour break was held fair in *Tait v South Yorkshire PTE* (1979) COIT 939/241. Despite Tait's five years of good service, it was held that there was a clear safety rule prohibiting the consumption of alcohol on pain of summary dismissal, and the employers had to enforce this strictly to prevent any laxity occurring. Logically of course, drunkenness which leads to actual negligence by the employee, causing damage or injury, is even more likely to lead to a fair dismissal! In *Richardson v Teesside Farmers Oils Ltd* (1975) COIT 335/116, Richardson, while drunk allowed a woman colleague to drive his loaded oil tanker on the highway. She collided with a wall, causing minor damage, and Richardson was dismissed. This was held to be fair, because Richardson was breaking the law, putting fellow employees at risk, causing damage and risking his employer's operator's licence.

The stress on safety can extend even to penalizing senior staff who fail to report the drunken, unsafe behaviour of subordinates, or to act against it. The management, in *Williams v Ciba Plastics* (1981) 87/81 EAT, specifically warned managers to prevent drinking at Christmas, an offence incurring summary dismissal. Williams, a senior manager, discovered drinking, but did not attempt to find the culprits until after the holiday. His dismissal was held to be fair since the employer was entitled to expect effective action from senior staff in carrying out the safety policy.

Drunkenness on and off duty

Usually such matters will be covered by safety or disciplinary rules. With off-duty drinking, the fairness of the dismissal will often depend on the importance of the individual's position, that is, if he performs key duties or is in the public eye. It was held, in *Entwistle v British Airways Board* (1979) COIT 930/60 that, though Entwistle was out of uniform when flying to join his plane, the abusive incidents he caused would damage British Airways' customer image, and his dismissal was fair. However, in the case of *Gardner v Morgan Trust Co of New York* (1981) COIT 1181/188, although the employee became drunk and abusive, it was the custom to allow drinking on an employee's birthday, and it was felt that management had not only condoned such drinking but had not explained that the employee would be subject to dismissal if he did become drunk. Gardner's dismissal was held to be unfair, though the compensation was reduced by 75 per cent.

Possession of alcohol at work

Employers often have rules against unauthorized possession of alcohol either on safety grounds, or to prevent pilfering, as established by *The Distillers Company v Gardner* (1982) IRLR 47. Again, the approach to these rules should not be inflexible, as, if the amount is small, the tribunals will normally dismiss this as *de minimis*. An example of this is *Scottish Grain Distillers Ltd v McNee* (1982) EAT 34/82 where the possession of a small quantity of 1 per cent ethyl alcohol was held not to merit dismissal.

In the absence of rules concerning alcohol possession, employers should be most wary of dismissing for mere possession, without having given previous warnings, as this is most likely to result in unfair dismissal.

Absence without leave and lateness

These are probably the most common effects of drinking and are, under employment law, treated as misconduct. There are three types of this offence.

1 The first is a long absence to recover from a chronic bout of drinking. But the fact that an employee has not been seen for weeks does not entitle the employer to argue a 'constructive resignation'. Instead, he must find out why the absence has occurred and either give formal notice of dismissal, or keep the contract open and consider rehabilitating the employee back into the organization. In these cases, the initiative is always with the employer.

If, however, the bout makes the performance of the contract impossible into the foreseeable future, the employer may seek to argue that the contract is frustrated by an unforeseen event. Whether heavy drinking leading to incapacity is indeed an unforeseen event through no fault of either party may be questioned, though it could be analogous to imprisonment and treated as a long-term illness (eg *Norris v Southampton City Council* (1982) and *Egg Store Ltd v Leibovic* (1977)).

2 The second type is an unacceptable level of minor absences, especially where these are certified as something else, but with the employer suspecting their real cause. Guidance on how to respond is given by the EAT in *International Sports Company Ltd v Thompson* (1980) IRLR 340. There should be a fair review of the employee's attendance record and his reasons for absence. If they are due to chronic drinking, then sickness procedures should be used. If the drinking is sporadic, the employer should give the employee a chance to explain, begin the warnings procedure, and provide a chance for improvement. If there is no improvement, the employer may proceed to dismissal. Any persistent indisposition due to hangovers should be treated in the same way and, obviously, much reliance will be placed on the employer's monitoring procedures.

3 The third type of misconduct relates to being absent without leave or late entering work, returning from lunch or leaving early in order to drink. This can easily be covered by straightforward disciplinary rules which are clearly communicated to the workforce. The absence of such rules or a written policy may make dismissal for a first offence appear excessive, particularly if the employer has condoned drinking during working hours, as in *Foy v Johnson & Johnson Ltd* (1981) COIT 1206/142. Here shiftworkers who were found drinking in the firm's social club before the end of a shift were dismissed under a rule prohibiting the possession of alcohol on the premises. It was held to be unreasonable to invoke the rule when the employer provided the club's alcohol but, as leaving the shift early was considered a serious offence, compensation was reduced by 60 per cent.

Safety at Work

We have touched upon the importance of safety rules from the viewpoint of dismissal and we might now briefly consider the significance of such rules as regards claims against the employer. Broadly speaking, this raises questions under civil law as to the duty of the employer to provide a safe system of work for his employees and not to be vicariously liable, through the employee's negligence, to third parties. There is also a potential criminal liability under statutes such as the Health and Safety at Work Act 1974.

First the civil law. This requires, for a safe system of work, that the employer takes all reasonable precautions against reasonably foreseeable risks. This is a duty owed to all employees in the course of their employment, and will be broken if the employer fails to achieve a reasonable standard of care, causing damage, that is, injury. In essence, the duty may be broken down into five components:

1 a duty to provide safe and competent staff
2 a duty to provide a proper system of working which includes instruction, supervision and safety campaigns
3 a duty to provide safe premises
4 a duty to provide safe working equipment, which for most purposes is covered by the Employer Liability (Defective Equipment) Act 1969, giving an automatic right of action against an employer
5 a duty to provide safety equipment

Usually, with an alcohol-related problem the first two sub-duties are of most significance. What we have already established about monitoring is important in determining whether an employee with a drink problem is still safe and competent in his work. The employer will be required to take reasonable steps to ascertain a foreseeable risk and, if there is *actual* knowledge of a person's drinking or alcoholism, then *so much greater* is the requirement that the employer overcome the risk. Thus an employee who, when drunk, will pick fights, act irresponsibly or override safety devices should be dealt with to ensure no repetition of his actions because there would then exist actual knowledge of his propensity to become drunk and unsafe. Note again, that the duty is not towards the individual, but his workmates.

The definition of reasonable precaution, bearing in mind the law of dismissal, obviously depends on the seriousness of the risk. Two main tactics could be pursued. The first would be to remove the individual completely through dismissal, or suspension, or transfer to other duties. The second tactic would be to increase supervision, perhaps ensuring further training, and certainly, in the case of an alcohol-related problem allowing the opportunity for rehabilitation. However, the greater the risk of death or serious injury implied in retaining the individual in post and the more costly and disruptive this line becomes, the more likely is it that a reasonable precaution will mean the removal of that individual.

If an accident occurs through the drunken negligence of an employee, then the injured fellow employee may bring a claim against the employer. The *Employer's Liability (Compulsory Insurance) Act 1969* requires employers to carry insurance policies of £2 million against such claims and, although insurance companies bear the brunt of the claim, subsequent increased premiums refer the cost back to the employer. It may be that, under pressure from the insurers, the employer will successfully defend a claim on the grounds that there has been a breach of duty. This leaves the injured party with only one option, to sue the negligent employee for personal liability, which is not a good option at all!

If the drunken employee is injured, then he might also sue the employer for failure under one or more of the sub-duties given above. However, he is likely to be met with a partial defence of contributory negligence, which would reduce damages, or even *volenti non fit injuria.* This latter is more difficult as it depends on the drunken employee having consented to the risk run and that this is not a risk which is inherent in the work (eg *ICI v Shortwell* (1965) AC 656). The extent to which a habitually drunken employee consents to anything is open to question, but by and large the employer has a minimal 'duty' to protect employees against themselves.

For third parties injured or damaged by the acts of a drunken employee, the alternatives are either to sue the individual or, more feasible, to sue the employer for vicarious liability. This latter recourse is generally not available for the drunken acts of independent contractors (but cf. *McArdle v Andmac Roofing* 1WR 356 1967), as there is theoretically no control over the manner of their performance. The action is dependent on two points, the first that a tortious act was committed by the drunken employee, the second that it was committed in the course of employment. It is the latter point which can cause difficulties because, if the act is done purely for the employee's own benefit and is unrelated to his work, there will be no vicarious liability. The question which is asked is "Was the employee doing what he was paid to do, even though in a careless, disobedient, dishonest or other wrongful way?"

If the employee was not doing something for the benefit of the employer, but was, instead, on a 'frolic of his own', then vicarious liability will not apply. Thus, in *Hilton v Burton Ltd* (1961) 1 AU E.R. 74, demolition workers were allowed to use the firm's van for obtaining lunchtime food. Two of them used it to go drinking and then on to a cafe. As a result of negligent driving, one was killed. It was held that no vicarious liability existed because they were 'on a frolic of their own' and not doing something they were employed to do, or which was for the benefit of the employer. On the other hand, if the employer controlled the journey, by providing the transport, imposing rules of use and conduct and requiring certain functions to be performed, then vicarious liability would exist because it would reasonably be considered incidental to the employee's work.

Criminal law, that is principally statute law, also imposes wide duties on the employer to provide a safe system of work. The Health and Safety at Work Act 1974 S.2(2) imposes a general duty to use care as far as is reasonably practicable on the employer. In effect, it repeats the common law duty of care examined above, though with criminal sanctions of unlimited fines and up to two years' imprisonment. More likely, however, such a duty will lead initially to improvement or to prohibition notices from the Health and Safety Executive inspectorate (Health and Safety at Work Act 1974 SS21 and 22). Under S.2(3) a further obligation is placed on the employer requiring a written statement of safety policies. It is here that the employer may wish to demonstrate his determination to implement an alcohol policy along the lines already discussed.

Through the establishment of safety committees and safety representation, a channel will exist for agreement on such matters between workforce and management. Furthermore, some industries adopt voluntary Codes of Safety Practice, as in the chemicals industry, which ought to be complied with and which would be considered of evidential value in any legal action, either criminal or civil.

For the employee, the Health and Safety at Work Act does introduce an obligation of responsibility under SS7 and 8. The first provision requires the employee not only to take reasonable care of his own safety but that of others, and to co-operate with the employer to enable the employer to carry out his duties. This last requirement goes further than the old equivalent provision in the Factories Act 1961 S.143. It could, for example, be interpreted as requiring individuals to comply with an alcohol policy if that policy were necessary for the employer's duty under S.2(2). It could certainly be used to cajole employees into accepting reasonable rehabilitation programmes to ensure that they were no longer a danger. One aspect of alcohol abuse and isolated drunkenness is a disregard for safety equipment or even an intentional removal of such equipment. Thus though the employer must carry out his S.2 duty or duties under other legislation (Factories Act 1961 SS12-14) to ensure that such behaviour does not occur, this will not absolve the employee from his duty under S.8 not to interfere with safety equipment, especially if injury results. The degree to which the Health and Safety Executive is likely to prosecute in such cases is still an unknown quantity. On past Factories Act experience, it is likely to be minimal, with the employer bearing the brunt of the inspectorate's concern.

Future Trends

The most obvious trend, stemming largely from the material on unfair dismissal, is the putting into effect of the type of alcohol policy in industry which is suggested in the section on the problem drinker at work. This policy should be agreed between management, unions and employees, and be applied to all staff levels. The procedures it contains should place less emphasis on the disciplinary aspects of a case and stress capability and rehabilitation. In doing this, it should be tailored towards the size and administrative resources of the particular organization in which it is to operate. Whatever else, fair procedures in accordance with the IPM Guide (Appendix 1 below) should be adopted.

Such an alcohol policy should provide for the identification of problem drinkers, for appropriate intervention in the situation and allow for the treatment of such drinkers, especially through the maintenance of confidentiality, job security and the provision of sick leave. Essentially, the law of unfair dismissal stresses the necessity of the employer taking a positive view so that rehabilitation of the employee may occur whenever possible.

The second trend runs somewhat counter to this, as it means the use of the law, through its safety provisions, as a preventative. In part, pressure for this may come as a result of the ever-increasing sums paid in damage compensation for negligence and the pressure is applied by the employer's insurers, who generally foot the bill and only partially recoup their losses through increased premiums.

Undoubtedly, if there were ever to be established a 'no-fault' compensation scheme, then criminal law measures would become permanent. It would become a question of degree, that is, the extent to which an employer should be made criminally vicariously liable; or whether there should exist a criminal offence of being intoxicated at work, irrespective of risk or danger, as under the more draconian Criminal Code of the DDR (East Germany). It would call into further debate the use of breathalysers or other objective biological testing, with their obvious evidential advantage over subjective judgement, but with their perceived disadvantage in terms of industrial relations.

Whatever the trend, one might say it will be fair and dry.

The Law and Drugs in the Workplace

Much of the approach of Employment Law and the development of workplace policy described in relation to alcohol problems ought to apply equally to drug abuse and addiction. There is, however, a fundamental difference which affects the decisions of employers and tribunals alike in such matters: the use or supply of unprescribed drugs (unlike drinking in itself) may amount to a criminal offence, subject to statutory exceptions. As a result, Employment Law, as reflected in the limited number of tribunal cases, tends to lay great stress upon drugs use being treated as misconduct rather than reflecting upon the capability of the individual employee concerned.

An employer who knowingly continued to employ a person with a drugs problem could be liable under criminal law if he or she knew that illegal drugs were being used on the premises, not only from the viewpoint of the Misuse of Drugs Act 1971 but also in failing to provide a safe system of work under the Health and Safety at Work Act 1974. These points are, of course, in addition to the probable breach of common-law duties of safety, owed to fellow employees and third parties, which may arise in the event of accidents and injuries arising from the actions of a drug-taking employee.

There are two aspects which are paramount in a general consideration of Employment Law matters. The first is drug addiction or dependency affecting the capability of an employee. The second is misconduct involving the use of drugs.

Drug use affecting the capability of the employee

This should logically be treated in the same way as an alcohol policy would suggest. Quite simply, rehabilitation would be a primary aim. To justify this, one should consider whether the work environment had contributed to or exacerbated the condition; the extent of the costliness and disruption of losing an otherwise reliable employee; and whether a tribunal would consider one's actions to be a reasonable response by an employer to the problem. However, industrial tribunals have shown a preference for treating drug use and addiction as misconduct (for example, see *Walton v TAC Construction Materials* below). Only rarely have employees been considered sympathetically, usually where medical treatment is involved.

Thus, in *London Regional Transport v Burke* EAT 726/84, a ticket collector failed to record excess fares on two occasions, having obtained them from two LRT 'testers'. The collector had been undergoing medical drug treatment. She was dismissed for gross misconduct. It was held that she was unfairly dismissed because a reasonable employer would not have taken the hard line of summary dismissal, particularly in view of the Welfare report on her domestic circumstances and drug treatment. Even so, her compensation order was reduced by 25 per cent because of her contributory conduct.

Employers may usually seek to avoid any potential personnel problems by adopting a policy of not employing drug users. Refusal to engage an individual on grounds that there is potential incapability because of drug dependency is legitimate. Furthermore, the employer may seek systematically to dismiss drug addicts or users, this being considered by tribunals to be within a range of 'reasonable responses' for employers dismissing someone on grounds of 'conduct'. For example, in *Walton v TAC Construction Materials* (1981 LRLR 357, Walton was dismissed after 13½ months when it was discovered that he was addicted to heroin. Prior to employment he had not disclosed his addiction on an application form. During his employment he had undertaken treatment to reduce his addiction by substituting to diconal. He admitted to the employer that he was a registered drug addict and was summarily dismissed on the ground of his misconduct, specifically that he had obtained employment by deception and that his addiction contravened Company policy against engaging addicts. The tribunal held that he was fairly dismissed: it was within a reasonable range of responses in accordance with an entirely reasonable policy of not employing drug adicts. This was despite the apparent lack of investigation into Walton's individual circumstances. Interestingly, on this latter point the decision of *Polkey v A.E. Dayton Services Ltd* (1988) ICR 142 might have found this to be procedurally unfair post-1987.

Of course, the Rehabilitation of Offenders Act 1974 does produce some limitation upon the ability of employers to require information relating to 'spent' convictions of drug offences and provides protection against dismissal for failure to inform the employer, provided it is within the definition of a 'spent' offence. Thus, in *Hendry v Scottish Liberal Club* (1977) IRLR 5 an earlier conviction for possession of cannabis was, in part, used to justify the summary dismissal of Hendry. The tribunal held that it was an unfair dismissal because his conviction was spent under S1 of the Rehabilitation of Offencers Act. Under S4(3) it was an inadmissible ground for dismissing him. If there are mutliple grounds for dismissal, the rule is that all must be capable of reaching the standard of fairness (*Smith v City of Glasgow District Council,* 1987, IRLR 326) for the employer to succeed in his defence.

Misconduct involving the use of drugs both at work and outside employment

If the employer intends to rely upon the reason of misconduct, then the burden will be upon him, or her to show, typically, either that there was a breach of company rules, or that drug taking had caused an accident or safety risk, or that it gave rise to violent or abusive behaviour. Once the reason is established, the tribunal will consider whether the employer has acted fairly and reasonably in the circumstances. This will include consideration of whether there are rules or a company policy against drug taking; whether these are connected to a disciplinary procedure supported by warnings; whether an adequate investigation has been carried out, with opportunities for the employee to draw the employer's attention to further explanations, arguments and mitigating circumstances; and finally, whether the decision to dismiss was within a range of reasonable responses by the employer.

Some of the factors which are considered by the tribunal on this latter point include:

(i) whether or not the conduct was on- or off-duty and the effect that it might have upon the employer's reputation and business to be linked with illegal activities
(ii) the actual or potential effects upon safety at work
(iii) whether or not the behaviour complained of was incompatible with the employee's position of responsibility eg if working with children or other vulnerable groups
(iv) whether or not there are mitigating circumstances.

Company policy and rules

Some companies, as maintained above, have taken the view that they will not employ drug users as a matter of company policy, and it is often sufficient for an employer to argue that the dismissal was in pursuance of such a policy. Although there are few examples of employer's drafting rules against drug use, it is obviously part of good management practice to have such express rules and to draw these and their disciplinary consequences to the attention of the workforce. However, employees are expected to know that criminal conduct of this type is prohibited implicitly, for example in *Anderson v Oak Motor Works* (1982) COIT 1270/153, where a dismissal was held to be fair for smoking cannabis at work despite the absence of any express rule. Despite this, it is wise, particularly if dealing with off-duty drug use, to include express prohibitory rules in the contract of employment.

Interview, investigations and warnings

As a consequence of the Polkey case, emphasis upon procedural fairness in terms of interviews to obtain explanations from the employee and thorough investigation of the facts have become paramount. Thus in *Tabor v Mid-Glamorgan CC* (1981) COIT 1165/7, for example, the employee concerned had been convicted of growing cannabis (perhaps in the mistaken belief that it was grass!). He did not smoke it although he did not believe it should be outlawed. Despite his conviction, it was considered that an insufficient investigation which would have ascertained that he did not use the drug, had been carried out. He was nonetheless fairly dismissed because of his position of responsibility as a teacher with teenage pupils.

In another unreported case, *British Airways Board v Davis* (1980) EAT 139/80, an airline steward with eight and a half years' excellent service was dismissed after conviction for forging prescriptions for amphetamines ('speed'), which he used to counteract tiredness brought on by his duties on long-haul flights. He was dismissed on grounds that the employer's reputation would be prejudiced and that drug-taking incapacitated him in the performance of his duties. This was despite the fact that BA's own doctors' reports indicated that the drug had no side effects and that the medical effect of the drug on Davis should have been further investigated. It was held to be an unfair dismissal: the reasonable employer should have made those further medical investigations prior to dismissal.

It appears that it is insufficient for the employer to rely merely upon the fact that the employee has been arrested and charged. Investigation by the employer is still required. Thus, in *Ladup Ltd v Barnes* (1982) ICR 107, Barnes was dismissed from a job in a casino after being charged with growing and possessing cannabis. No investigation was carried out nor was any real opportunity provided for him to provide an explanation. It was held that this was an unfair dismissal based simply upon the fact that Barnes had been charged. However, on appeal his compensation was reduced by 100 per cent due to his contributory fault (ie he was subsequently convicted!).

If the employer has grounds for believing that the employee is misusing drugs, then for first and minor offences it may be more appropriate to begin issuing warnings in accordance with a disciplinary procedure rather than dismissing him or her at once. When the warnings have been exhausted, there is nothing to prevent the employer dismissing for a further act of drugs misconduct. For example, in *Appolinari v Yorks Area Health Authority* (1980) COIT 977/232, the applicant had been given a formal warning after a drugs conviction, whilst a student nurse, that a further conviction would lead to dismissal. He was held to be fairly dismissed when convicted a second time. This was because the reputation of the hospital would be seriously affected; as a nurse, he was in a position of responsibility and trust towards his patients which would be compromised by conviction.

Factors to be considered within the range of reasonable responses
One particular consideration influencing the approach of the employer is whether the misconduct has occurred off-duty or not. Drug-taking outside of work is usually drawn to the attention of the employer when the employee is charged or convicted. The approach of the tribunals is a little less severe towards employees in that it will only be fair to dismiss for such off-duty conduct if the conviction damages the employer's reputation and business or if it makes him or her unacceptable to colleagues. Otherwise, the tribunal may well accept mitigating circumstances from the employee and decide in his or her favour.

Thus, in *Norfolk County Council v Bernard* (1979) IRLR 220, Bernard was a drama teacher who spent most of his employment instructing teachers and only occasionaly teaching teenagers. He was convicted of possessing cannabis after a few leaves were found in his car. He was dismissed on grounds that he was unsuitable to teach teenagers as a result of the conviction. The EAT found that he had been unfairly dismissed because the evidence revealed that he had smoked only two or three 'joints' several months before and had forgotten about the leaves. He had no interest in smoking cannabis and was morally opposed to drug-taking. He was shown to be of a high moral character and to be highly competent in his work. The conviction arose out of a single incident of foolishness, not vice, and was unlikely to affect the reputation of the employer; the dismissal was an excessive response which failed to take account of such mitigating elements.

The above case points to a primary consideration of the employer with regard to both off-duty and on-duty acts of drugs misconduct. The attitude of the public and the general belief that seemingly to condone drug offences (by retaining the employee) damages the image of the employer as a trustworthy and competent provider of services may be accepted by tribunals as strong grounds for dismissal. If the case does not seem to attract publicity, as in Davis' and Bernard's cases, then tribunals are less willing to agree with the employer and may instead consider mitigating circumstances which probably favour the employee. However, once the criminal case attracts press attention and becomes part of the public domain, the employer may show that public confidence is affected.

For example, in *Gunn v British Waterways Board* (1981) EAT 138/81, Gunn was demoted for a series of cannabis convictions. He was subsequently dismissed after conviction for stealing money and drugs. The latter conviction was publicized in a local newspaper which named his employers. The EAT held that although the offence was unlikely to interfere with his menial work as a lock-keeper, his employers were entitled to protect their reputation as responsible employers of labour.

Thus, the public perception of particular groups of workers such as nurses (the Appolinari case), teachers (Tabor's case) and air-traffic controllers (*Booth v Southampton Airport Ltd,* 1982, COIT 1276/230), may dictate that these workers should be of the highest integrity and reliability and free of blemish – and most certainly that they should not challenge legality. The fact that a criminal offence is committed is then seen as an additional secondary element to the major factor of damage to the employer's reputation and business integrity, something which is threatened by the very act of drugs use or possession.

A second major consideration is safety. The obligation on the employer under both the civil and criminal law (notably the Health and Safety at Work Act 1974) to ensure a safe system of work means that a proven safety risk will provide a fair reason, under misconduct or breach of an enactment, for dismissal. (However, this does not mean that employers need not pay attention to procedural fairness by investigating the circumstances etc, as outlined above.)

Thus, in *Anderson & Chambers v Oak Motor Works Ltd* (1982) COIT 1270/153, the two applicants were found at work smoking cannabis in a workshop where they were rebuilding engines. They were in an advanced state of intoxication. They were dismissed on grounds of incapability of performing their tasks and the more serious charge of being intoxicated near moving machinery and tanks of chemicals, thereby endangering themselves and others. The dismissal for gross misconduct was held to be fair because it was a reasonable response to a flagrant breach of safety standards and the open illegality of their action. Some occupations not only need to be safe, but need to be seen to be safe. For example, in *Booth v Southampton Airport Ltd,* an air-traffic controller was dismissed when it was discovered that he smoked cannabis outside his hours of duty. Despite evidence indicating that he was at all times fully competent and capable it was held to be a fair dismissal: public confidence in the safety of the service had to be maintained and so the employee had to be seen to be safe and the employers perceived to be taking no risks whatsoever.

Thirdly, tribunals will carefully consider the employer's response in special circumstances when the employee is in contact with children, has influence over vulnerable groups such as patients or is in a position of responsibility, and when their behaviour is incompatible with that status.

If there is contact with children, tribunals see this as a major factor justifying dismissal, especially where the employee may exercise influence over the children, in the case of a teacher. For example, teachers are expected not to show a total disregrd for the law, and certainly not in the context of drugs (as in Tabor's case).

Similarly, if the employee has influence over other groups which might be persuaded by his or her behaviour, this will be prominent in justifying dismissal. Thus, a nurse working with mental patients (Appolinari's case) and a seaman supervising young recruits were fairly dismissed because of their potential for influencing their charges by their behaviour in committing criminal offences (*Stanton v Atlantic Steam Navigation Co.*, 1977, COIT 701/97).

It may well happen that the employee's behaviour in using drugs or even condoning such misconduct is considered incompatible with the position of responsibility held. Thus, the administering of LSD to unsuspecting friends was seen as evidence to justify dismissal that the employee was irresponsible and thus generally unfit to be in charge of children at a swimming bath (*Freeman v Liverpool Corporation,* 1974, COIT 275/140).

Furthermore, in *Seddon v St Helens YMCA* (1982) COIT 1312/18, a night porter of a YMCA hostel allowed strangers into the hostel and permitted them to use drugs, according to residents' reports. After a full investigation, and despite denials by Seddon, he was dismissed; this was held to be a fair dismissal because Seddon's job was to ensure that the premises were protected and that the young people there were provided with a safe environment. He had shown a failure to justify the trust and responsibility placed upon him, by condoning such criminal acts.

The element of responsible behaviour is of particular importance for those employees involved in the legitimate dispensing or distribution of prescribed drugs, such as nursing staff (eg Khanum v Glamorgan AHA, 1978, IRLR 215) or chemists. Thus in *Stentiford v Goodalls Chemists* (1982) COIT 1313/29, Stentiford was a trainee dispenser who was anxious about her weight. She approached five doctors in turn to obtain prescriptions for amphetamines, a series of deceptive acts. She also approached a 'pusher'. When her employer discovered this, they sought advice from the Professional Association of Pharmacists, which indicated that she should not be allowed near controlled drugs. She refused alternative work and was dismissed. This was held to be fair: she had broken the trust and confidence that existed between herself and her employer. In such positions a high standard of behaviour and responsibility was essential.

Finally, any mitigating circumstances ought to be considered in determining whether the employer's response of dismissal was reasonable. Thus, if the job itself has caused the drug use (as it did in the Davis case), the employer should not immediately dismiss without exploring the possibility of alternatives such as rehabilitation or transfer.

Another example where additional consideration was required by the employer is *Burns v Dart Pleasure Craft:* Burns began smoking cannabis, he claimed, because of domestic and matrimonial difficulties which eventually caused a marriage break-up. He had agreed to give up the drug. He was still dismissed. It was held to be an unfair dismissal. A reasonable employer would have given him an ultimatum and waited to see whether he succeeded especially as he would not be required to take vessels out to sea for the next few months and would thus not be exposing the public to any risk from his drug-taking.

Chapter Six
The Personnel Implications

Steve Palmer and Fred Dickenson

Introduction

We are sure that the foregoing chapters will have given the personnel management reader some pause for thought. One great difficulty we ourselves had to overcome was our own attitude to alcohol and drug misuse. Particularly the view that, whereas alcohol misuse was a misfortune which may afflict anyone, drug misuse was the problem of social outcasts who deserved neither sympathy nor help.

Yet the attitudes that have led to this divorce between the amount of help to alcohol misusers as opposed to their drug-using counterparts seems of fairly recent arrival. After all, it was only one hundred and thirty years ago that Britain fought with the Chinese for the right to trade opium in the Far East. Indeed, when one working-party member claimed 'Victorian attitudes' to drugs and drug users, he was surprised to learn that Victorians had a comparatively liberal attitude to drug use and were much more concerned by the alcohol problem of the time. Part of their concern with alcohol misuse – bearing in mind that drug use was very much the preserve of the higher social classes – was based on the misery it caused to families; but equal concern related to the effects that working-class over-indulgence had on productivity.

Over the years we have seen an important change in attitude, although people are far more likely to shun a woman with a substance-misuse problem than they would a man. Drinking is seen as a great social activity and any attempts to equate alcohol consumption with drug use are dismissed as special pleading. The result is there for all to see, with rising levels of drinking and associated levels of violence, crime and general anti-social behaviour. It therefore no longer seems to make sense to isolate drug users from the help that employers can and should provide.

We have published this guide to substance misuse, therefore, because we believe that there is little real difference in the problems caused by alcohol and drug misuse or the remedies for them. Of course we accept that drug use is dangerous and should be discouraged, but we do not believe that discouragement is aided by hysteria which leads those that could help to turn their backs. On the other hand, perhaps attitudes to drink could do with a little more 'hysteria' to bring the problem into its true perspective. All this comes at a time when, whilst many drugs are illegal and their possession means heavy fines or imprisonment, licensing laws are amended to extend opening hours.

These different attitudes are often reflected in the policies on substance misuse that employers adopt. Whilst we could find many examples of alcohol-misuse policies, there were very few that related to drug misuse (some indication, perhaps, of the relative size of these problems). Even where drugs were included under the policy, quite often the understanding and help offered to those with alcohol problems – time off, counselling, protection of rights etc, compared favourably with the stark and often only option facing the illegal drug user – dismissal. The difference is further underlined where pre-employment testing is concerned. We discuss the whole issue of testing later on, but it was by no means unusual to find an employer, whose policy stated that what employees did in their own time was their own business provided it did not affect their credibility and ability to do the job, also included testing for drugs as part of the pre-employment medical.

Even with the single-issue policies, employers differ as to what they are dealing with. Some say that alcohol misuse is an illness, others that it is more akin to sickness except that it is self-afflicted, whilst others label it "selfish and self-indulgent". The initial attitude determines the policy, ranging from the sympathetic, where alcohol is perceived as an illness, to the disciplinarian, where it appears 'self-indulgent'. The treatment that employees can get for alcohol problems therefore varies from employer to employer.

We feel that attitudes are the major problem in dealing with substance misuse. The personnel manager clearly has a major role in the beginning to bring the attitudes of people up to date by the provision of information that is helpful and positive. We would not presume to suggest that there is any one policy approach to this issue; we would argue, however, that we all need to get our act together to ensure a fair and effective approach to substance misuse in the workplace. This book and the Guide that goes with it (see Appendix 1) represent our contribution to that process.

Why a substance-misuse policy?

If we turn back to Chapter 2 the following extracts should give any employer cause for thought:

> . . . [the evidence suggests] that 10 per cent of drinking males [have alcohol] problems at work
>
> Of the 48 employees referred for help over a four-year period [in a large engineering concern], 32 had industrial accidents in the three-year period prior to referral. The company safety manager estimated that this was 50 per cent higher than the workforce average.
>
> Overall, drinkers take four times as many days off work as other workers . . . It is estimated that 8-14 million days are lost each year as a result of excessive drinking.
>
> It has been conservatively estimated that the total resource costs [of alcohol misuse] in England and Wales at 1987 prices is about £2 billion.
>
> The CBI, in its document *Danger – Drugs at Work*, quotes a figure of 25 per cent of those presenting to agencies with a drugs problem as being in full-time employment.

The working environment reflects society at large and to this extent it is only reasonable to expect every employer to have employees on their staff with an alcohol problem; they are less likely to find someone with a drugs-related problem but the odds increase with the size of organization.

Why is it that employers seem prepared to turn a blind eye to an activity which collectively costs them almost £800 million a year in sickness absence alone?

All of the personnel and occupational health specialists we spoke to had some horrific stories to tell. Everyone had at least one 'Old Joe' who was a good enough worker in the morning but to whom it was wiser not to give hard, dangerous or important work after lunch. Managers who don't return from lunch until after 3pm are apparently fairly commonplace; as are the employees who turn a blind eye to the open drinking of a colleague and willingly (or, if not willingly, uncomplainingly) take on the extra work.

Basically, people do not like to 'shop' a colleague. This attitude is compounded by the common view that drunkenness is embarrassing, daring or amusing, and not to cover up for it would somehow be acting as a killjoy. That covering up may ultimately lead to the destruction of families or friendships or even the death of the colleague (and, occasionally, innocent bystanders) does not enter into the calculation.

In purely hard-headed terms, employers need a substance-misuse policy to help minimize the loss of production resulting from the misuse of drugs or alcohol and to help meet safety requirements. Of course, dismissal is an option but, as we have seen, would probably amount to unreasonable behaviour by the employer if efforts had not been made to solve the problem some other way. In any event, dismissal involves throwing away money and expertise and wasting a resource which need not be wasted.

But, if the business cost is enormous, so is the social cost. Many employers state that what an employee does off their premises in their own time is purely the individual's responsibility. This is not a philosophy that many of them seem prepared to accept when it comes to drug use, however. It is never that simple to divorce cause and effect. An employee who drinks heavily in the evening may or may not come into work the following morning with a hangover; they may or may not have domestic troubles; and they may or may not be heading for long-term and expensive health problems. The point is that all of those factors may affect work performance and therefore the link between drinking, albeit in leisure time, and work is stronger than many employers are prepared to accept.

Our thesis is that, whether a substance-misuse exists for 'hard-nosed' or soft-nosed' reasons, it amounts to the same thing – that the healthy employee is the best performer and recurring substance misuse, no matter when it occurs, is usually the sign of an unhappy employee.

Finally, there are questions of image and responsibility. Most employers accept nowadays that substance misuse is a health problem. Some would argue that it is, in itself, an illness, although this view now finds less support. What matters is it deserves to be treated like any other health problem – with full access to the sick-pay scheme, job preservation and all rights maintained – the only difference often being the possible involvement of the disciplinary procedure to stop backsliding. Having a substance-misuse policy forms part of a good employer's image (although, interestingly, few employers seem keen to have their policy widely known by the public at large lest people assume that their staff are all alcoholics, drug pushers etc.). Some employers argue that the cost of the policy might be prohibitive, although the expense will certainly be less than expected for the reasons outlined on page 26. In any event, one major employer has estimated that two rehabilitations a year easily pay for the policy. Tied in with the issue of image, employers must sometimes accept that they have some responsibility for any substance misuse amongst their staff. Pressure on employees to drink arising from their working environment comes from three main sources:

corporate culture
social milieu
stress

The *corporate culture* issue is one to which we intend to turn later, but is of sufficient importance for mention here. Some organizations' cultures encourage drinking – both on and off the premises. Reference back to page 17 and the table outlining the occupations most at risk suggests those industries most likely to have an 'alcohol culture'. But, even in industries less obviously affected, management may have a style that encourages drinking. In the finance sector, for instance, senior managers may well drink in the evenings with their subordinates (as anyone who has tried to get a drink in a City pub after 5.30pm can attest). Junior staff may feel psychologically that they cannot miss out on these events as they may come to be seen as 'not fitting in' or 'not the right sort for promotion' by their boss. We heard of companies where wives were complaining of their husbands returning home around midnight every night because of this form of 'social' drinking. In one case, a senior manager was himself a very heavy drinker, which added a new dimension to the evening sessions.

Then, of course, there is the lunch-time drinking resulting from the provision of bars on company premises or drink in the executive dining room. Given that two pints of beer would be the limit for most people if they wished to keep their driving licence, it seems strange that much of industry and commerce is quite happy for its senior staff to take important decisions after even moderate sessions in the company bar or dining-room – a generous attitude that it would be quite unprepared to extend to its shop-floor or clerical employees. The point is that some employers have a duty to provide an answer to alcohol misuse – and occasionally drug misuse – because they are part of the problem. But we would stress that a substance misuse policy should not just be about identifying individuals with problems and offering them help, but also about providing an environment which does not encourage drinking as a norm.

The *social milieu* is tied in with this issue of corporate culture. Small, highly skilled, departments will often reinforce their social values by drinking together. This is fine as far as it goes, but it often ceases to be a social event and becomes a chore as the pressure to drink every day with the same crowd increases. As we have noted, the pressure increases if the senior manager is involved in, or leads, the socializing.

Similarly, *stress* is an issue which is often work-related and which can lead to substance misuse. If the stress of a particular occupation cannot be reduced, employers should at least have policies intended to ensure that it does not lead to something worse.

We could conclude this section by drawing attention to the costs of not having a policy outlined in the anecdotal evidence on page 27. In a high technology company, the 20 worst drinkers were estimated to have cost the company £500,000 per year. A study in a large car manufacturing company showed that their alcohol and drugs policy had led to a 50 per cent fall in occupational injuries, 60 per cent in sickness and accident payments, 80 per cent in absenteeism, 40 per cent in lost time, and 50 per cent in grievances and disciplinary action.

These findings put the case for substance-misuse policies far more eloquently than we can.

What can employers do?

For all the reasons outlined in the preceding sections, the Institute believes that it is sound business sense for employers to introduce and maintain substance-misuse policies. What these policies should contain is outlined in greater detail in Chapter 3 and in the example policy given at Appendix 2, but the broad headings are as follows:

- assurances that help is available
- staff seeking help will be treated in confidence
- time-off requirements will be granted under the same terms and conditions as for sickness absence
- their jobs will, if possible, be kept open for them or alternative, equivalent employment found
- their terms and conditions will be no worse on return to work than when they left and service-related entitlements will be unaffected
- the role of the disciplinary procedure vis-à-vis the substance-misuse policy
- an after-care programme
- means of monitoring and evaluating the policy
- management and employee responsibilities

Drawing up the policy is one thing; of greater importance is the need to ensure that it is effective. This is an issue we address in the next section. Let us consider some of these policy issues in more depth.

Assurances that help is available
Most policies note that requests for help and/or referral usually come from three sources:

- self-referral – where the employee privately approaches their GP or one of the substance-misuse agencies, in which case the employer is not involved, although it may have happened because of his policy
- voluntary referral – where an employee is still working satisfactorily but is identified as possibly having a substance-misuse problem and is offered assistance under the policy

- mandatory referral – where the employee's performance is unsatisfactory and the supervisor/manager sends the employee for assessment and the disciplinary procedure may need to be invoked.

In the latter two cases, the policy will outline the type of help available. In the case of *voluntary referral* it is, naturally, up to the employee to contact the relevant agency often via the company medical adviser or personnel executive. The agency then asesses the problem and determines the programme for help and assistance. Liaison is maintained by the medical adviser with the agency.

Mandatory referral is slightly more complicated because the disciplinary procedure will often have been invoked. The manager will refer the employee to the medical adviser who then will contact the agency. Because of the involvement of the disciplinary procedure, the problem has to be addressed as to what to do if the employee refuses the referral or backslides on subsequent treatment. (In the case of *voluntary referral* these issues are not involved because performance has not fallen nor has the disciplinary procedure been invoked; employees are usually warned that they are responsible for maintaining performance and that this will be constantly monitored in future.) Generally, in cases both of refusal or backsliding, the disciplinary procedure, which is usually only suspended, will be used.

Employees will be treated in confidence

It goes without saying that an employee who voluntarily seeks help for a substance-misuse problem should be treated in confidence and although, by definition, a mandatory referral will be more widely known the same 'in confidence' treatment should apply.

The fact that many occupational health specialists are doctors raises issues of confidentiality between managers. Personnel specialists must accept that they will receive only the minimal information where an employee seeks help or is referred directly to the occupational health department. This arrangement is not ideal particularly if the disciplinary procedure is later invoked and personnel find themselves faced with a problem they did not know existed. Clearly, there is a problem here but, by and large, employees are entitled to the same levels of confidentiality that they would expect from their GP. Personnel managers should seek permission from the employee concerned if they wish to approach other bodies (internal and external) for information. The onus will be on the employee to give that permission.

Time off, job protection etc

Organization policies now argue that people with substance-misuse problems should be treated *as though they were sick*. By this process they are entitled to receive the normal benefits in respect of sick pay or sick leave as they would if off work for any illness-related problem.

By and large they would also expect to return to the same job with the same benefits, although most organizations include the right to provide equivalent employment if it is not inappropriate for the employee to return to their old job.

The role of the disciplinary procedure

The relationship between the disciplinary procedure and the substance misuse policy is often complex. Normally, the former backs up the latter, but, at the same time, it must not be seen to be a 'let out', or a means of 'bucking the system'.

The fear is always that some people with an alcohol problem could use, for instance, the referrals under the alcohol policy to avoid justifiable disciplinary action. To avoid this, most policies state that nothing in them negates the employer's right to discipline the employee.

The disciplinary procedure is kept in reserve both to encourage employees to accept referral and to keep them on course. Giving up a treatment course, or relapsing within twelve months of treatment does, under some policies, lead to a previously suspended disciplinary action being invoked. In some cases of gross misconduct the disciplinary procedure is invoked to provide for instant dismissal, No employer forgoes *in all circumstances* the right to dismiss. Even so, there is a need for clarity in the rules and for actions to be 'reasonable'.

There is one slight peculiarity in the treatment handed out to one-off offenders under policies. Someone who came to work drunk after a stag night might find themselves disciplined, whilst a colleague who had a known drinking problem was merely referred. This would appear a strange approach, but there is clearly little point in referring the one-off drinker who should perhaps have known better anyway. In any event, this anomalous situation is something which employers should be aware of.

Introducing a policy – the essentials

From our discussions with organizations it became clear that the successful introduction and operation of a substance-misuse policy required considerable effort at all stages of its development. From our researches we have distilled the following 'essentials' for success.

Consultation

No fundamental reason exists as to why a substance-misuse policy should be the sole property of the personnel department or, indeed, of management generally. In fact, the policy would probably be less effective if it were. The more that people are involved in drawing up the policy and implementing it, the more they will have ownership and a desire to see it work.

Four bodies seem to be most involved in drawing up a policy: management generally, occupational health department, personnel department and employees (via their representatives). No one said to us that getting the agreement of these four groups to either the need for a policy or its implementation was particularly difficult. In fact, the only general difficulty encountered usually stemmed from employees who tend to take a much more hard-nosed attitude to the possibility that the policy could be used by lead-swingers or malingerers. Some public sector bodies subject to control by elected members found much the same attitude irrespective of political persuasion.

The policy would normally be drafted first in very loose form by the personnel (and occupational health) department and mulled over in greater detail by a working party of management and employees. The major areas of potential disagreement centre on the treatment of referrals and the role of the disciplinary procedure. As we have noted above, the decision to treat referrals under the terms of the organizations' sick-pay scheme, and the use of disciplinary procedures generally to back up the policy, can help reduce contention.

In some areas, employees' representatives were not involved directly in the process – either because they were not unionized or because philosophically the organization did not see occupational health as a matter for negotiation or consultation. There are no reasons to believe that the operation of such substance-misuse policies suffer in this environment, although they certainly would where a union culture was stronger. Either way, the involvement of management outside the personnel and occupational health departments appears essential.

Communication

Following consultation there is the question of communication. In essence, three issues need to be communicated:

- the problems caused by alcohol and drug misuse both in society and the workplace and therefore the need for a substance-misuse policy
- the existence and operation of the organization's policy
- the desirability of voluntary referral from those in need of help

Obviously, the approaches and difficulties of getting these issues over to employees will be a function of size, diversity of operating units, work patterns etc. For these reasons it is as well to start the communications exercise well in advance. Communicating the nature and effects of substance misuse to raise awareness and interest in the issue can easily begin well before the policy is agreed. Raising awareness can be done via the normal communication channels that the organization has. In the public sector there tends to be a reliance on the written word but, as in other organizations, the use of videos, films, briefing groups and other presentations is growing. Some organizations issue to all employees short booklets on the issue in a cheerful and easily read form. Often this will include information on safe drinking limits and a 'diary' to help employees check their own weekly consumption. This clearly arouses interest.

Communicating the existence and content of the substance-misuse policy may be carried out in the same way, although greater involvement of management, particularly first-line management, in briefing employees helps to get the message over and to underline management's enthusiastic involvement in making the policy work.

Training

At the same time that the initial communications exercise takes place, organizations should be thinking about and implementing their training schedule. Considering the emphasis that most policies place on line management in identifying and referring potential substance misuses, and the foregoing view that communicating the policy should be a supervisory matter, this particular group must receive in-depth training.

One- or two-day courses are run in-house in most organizations to a programme generally devised and run by the outside agencies or personnel and occupational health departments.

The training sessions should be used to reinforce the message that substance misuse is a problem that management takes seriously and that the substance misuse policy underpins the organization's approach. Over a period of time all managers at whatever level should have received training. Even then, refresher courses and opportunities to exchange experiences about the operation of the policy should be provided.

Few organizations appear to make it mandatory that managers attend training sessions of this sort, but voluntary attendance is encouraged by senior management pressure. This brings us naturally to our fourth essential – commitment.

Commitment

The commitment of every one in the organization, but particularly the senior management to the policy is the backbone of making the policy work. This is one of the reasons that senior managers must be involved in the drafting and communicating of the policy and in ensuring that their junior management colleagues receive adequate training.

Commitment is not a one-off affair. All too often policies are introduced due to the enthusiasm of one member of the management team, only to atrophy when the driving force is removed by promotion, retirement or whatever. Long-term commitment requires continual pressure to ensure subordinates remain aware of the policy and are encouraged to use it. It means time off for training not once, but two or three times; and it requires that all new employees are made aware of the policy.

Managers might reasonably argue that they have other things to occupy them and, like many other policies, substance misuse comes well down their list of priorities. The emphasis must always be placed on how awareness about substance misuse and how to treat it can improve the bottom line.

Other issues

Whilst the foregoing four points are the 'essential essentials', there are some other issues whose existence seems to correlate with successful policies. These are:

- trust
- monitoring/record keeping
- revision

Trust operates in a number of directions. Clearly, there must be trust between the employee seeking help and the person(s) giving it that confidentiality will be maintained, that the employee really wants to be helped, that the policy will not be misused and so on. But it is also important that the various management groups trust each other and work well together. Line managers must be given the maximum support, otherwise they may see their position as the upholders of discipline being undermined by the 'do-gooders' in the personnel department. Personnel and occupation health managers must work together. We have found that in some organizations confidentiality post referral is an issue, in other it is not (it seems largely to depend on the attitude of the OHS staff); either way, there is clearly a case for working together on pre-referral matters and other issues.

No policy is perfect, certainly not at its inception, so there is always a need to *monitor* its operation. Keeping records allows its operation to be assessed, problems to be identified and experiences to be shared. Monitoring provides a valuable input to any subsequent *revisions*. As we learn more about substance misuse and as attitudes change, policies will need to keep up with the times. The initial step is to introduce a formal policy; it should not be written on tablets of stone.

What more?

All that has gone before in this book covers the current state of play on substance misuse in the workplace and the whys and in what manner organizations should go about dealing with it. What follows is more futuristic and is probably well in advance of most employers' thinking on the issue. If it reads like a Victorian temperance tract it is certainly not meant to, but some of the issues we address in this final section must be considered sooner or later.

First of all, we have already touched on the influence that the corporate culture has particularly on alcohol misuse. It seems hypocritical in the least to introduce a substance misuse policy whilst the executive dining-room continues to serve drinks before, after and during lunch, or when the company social club provides subsidized alcohol to the workforce. The message given to the average employee is confusing. "Yes, we have an alcohol misuse policy, but we are all sensible drinkers aren't we?" appears to be the management view. Yet, as we have suggested, it is likely that any workplace has at least one person with an alcohol problem. It is, perhaps, unfair that the many should suffer that the few be saved, but it is a fact of life (eg the compulsory wearing of seat-belts, the drink-driving laws, even member-only schemes at some football grounds). Organizations must sooner or later grapple with the inconsistencies in their approach to alcohol at work.

They must also grapple with their attitude to alcohol misuse out of work. Managers should be discouraged from having after-hours drinking sessions at which their subordinates are pressured to attend, or from the traditional Friday lunch-time binge. What individuals do in their spare time is their own affair certainly. Employers should, however, guard against cultural and environmental pressure that makes early evening drinking in the pub just an extension of the workplace. They must also consider their attitudes to alcohol misuse vis-à-vis drug misuse. Again their attitudes are likely to differ. The alcohol misuser can expect sympathetic, or if not sympathetic at least understanding treatment, whereas the user of illegal drugs faces dismissal. All this is notwithstanding the fact that a significant proportion of the population have tried an illegal drug at least once or that the damage caused by short-term drug use is far from clear. The Institute does not condone breaking the law or the use of drugs; it does, however, appear irrational to have one approach for the legal drug misuser – and alcohol is merely one type of drug – and another for the illegal misuser. The IPM would argue that, within the legal constraints on drug possession and the requirement on employers to ensure that illegal drugs are not brought onto their premises, the same policy should apply to all substance misusers alike.

Secondly, employers must start addressing the underlying problem that leads to substance misuse. This will almost certainly involve a more welfare-orientated approach. Whilst it has been our approach throughout this guide to argue the bottom-line importance of dealing with substance misuse, it is impossible to ignore the welfare aspects. A lot of substance misuse is unconnected with work and can arise from stress caused by bereavement, divorce, other family problems, or monetary difficulties.

Substance misuse is often the symptom of these stresses; addressing the misuse alone is unlikely to lead to any any long-term answer. Perhaps we need to invest more resources in welfare. One means of doing so is to make greater use of outside counselling agencies. Employers already often pay for counselling for those about to retire or be made redundant; why not extend this to employee assistance programmes?

All this costs money, of course, but it represents yet another measure of how seriously employers take their substance-misuse policies, which should form part of their overall policies on health.

Testing

Finally, we must comment on the issue of testing for drugs.

Some employers, usually subsidiaries of American concerns, have introduced testing for drugs into their pre-employment medicals. Failure to pass this test, now claimed to be so accurate that it can pin-point illegal drug use within the past thirty days, results in the job offer being withdrawn. That person cannot re-apply for a further twelve months.

This is an extremely delicate area. There are clearly advantages in testing: why should an employer knowingly take on someone who may have a drug problem? why should they put themselves at risk from their premises being used for taking illegal drugs? But in our view the disadvantages outweigh them.

First, tests of this sort might well be considered an infringement of individual liberty, particularly since most organizations take the view that what people do in their spare time is their own business. Secondly, a large proportion of calls made to SCODA (the Standing Conference on Drug Abuse) from drug users is about drug/blood levels and how long it takes particular drugs to work themselves out of the blood system. Armed with this knowledge, potential employees abstain from drugs before taking tests. Thirdly, some doubts have been cast on the accuracy of testing techniques which in any event may be picking up a one-off experiment with an illegal drug (bear in mind the high proportion of people who have tried drugs at least once) or, say, the passive smoking of someone who has been at a party where cannabis has been smoked. Fourthly, this is not the sort of information upon which recruitment decisions should be based, Finally, unless the test is carried out every thirty days what does it prove?

Conclusion

In its Seventy-fifth Anniversary Year the Institute is pleased to have worked with SCODA and Alcohol Concern to produce this guide. The Institute sincerely believes that employers should address the issues raised here and it hopes that this provocative and provoking statement of principles proves more useful than a bland reiteration of the material contained in many other excellent guides to substance misuse at work.

Appendix 1
Substance Misuse at Work: An IPM Guide

Introduction

This guide has been prepared by the Pay and Employment Conditions Committee of the Institute of Personnel Management, both to encourage the wider adoption of substance-misuse policies in the workforce and to help those personnel managers and others charged with introducing such policies and making them work . . .

That alcohol and drug misuse are major problems facing society is now accepted fact. Increasing concern has been expressed at all levels about rising alcohol and drug consumption and associated increases in violence and other anti-social behaviour. Whilst employers may like to think that this is an issue for society at large, they must take on some of the responsibility for solving it:

- because practically every employer will have some employees with an alcohol-related problem (and possibly a drug problem) on their staff, and
- to the extent that substance misuse may be the result of work pressures or corporate culture, employers could be seen as part of the problem
- it is the duty of every employer to maintain a safe and healthy working environment.

Employers have a unique contribution to make in helping people overcome substance-misuse problems. They have an influence over nearly half of an employee's waking time and can bring considerable pressure to bear via the 'carrot' of a sympathetic and caring approach to substance misusers and the 'stick' of discipline, or even dismissal, for those who turn down the offered help.

Some employers will still ask why they should put resources into programmes to deal with substance misuse. The answer is not totally, or even mostly, a moral one. Estimates suggest that around a quarter of all British men can be expected to experience some problems with alcohol misuse at some stage during their life; there is also concern being expressed at the increasing consumption of alcohol among women; a high proportion of these people with problems will be in employment. It is further estimated that 30 per cent of the under-40s have experimented with illegal drugs at one time or another and that some 25 per cent of drug users are in work. The total cost to employers from poor performance, absence and sick leave from these two sources has been put at between £600 and £800 million per year.

It does not make sense to turn a blind eye to this sort of wastage.

What is substance misuse?

Substance misuse can best be defined as the "problematic use of alcohol, drugs and other substances". Problematic use covers three main areas:

- *inappropriate use* where taking substances may aggravate an existing condition or situation that they were intended to ameliorate
- *habitual use* where an individual becomes so dependent on the effects of a drug (including alcohol) that the desire for these effects becomes a central and overriding concern of daily life, and has adverse occupational and social consequences
- *excessive use* which may lead to physical and psychological illness and could be fatal.

Sensible levels of alcohol intake are much lower than people think, being as little as 3 units per day for men (2 units for women) and even this intake should not be indulged in every day. A half pint of beer or a glass of wine constitutes 1 unit. With drugs, both legal and illegal, it is impossible to establish sensible dosages as the effects vary from drug to drug and person to person. Certainly drugs have the potential to change an individual's perception in a variety of ways – as indeed does alcohol – but this does not mean that an individual cannot function in his or her job.

Recognizing substance misuse

Substance misuse may be the cause or the symptom of a variety of problems at work. Clearly, the earlier that individuals with difficulties are identified the greater the likely success of any proffered assistance. All managers should maintain a constant check on the following aspects of their subordinates' work:

Absenteeism
Multiple unauthorized absences
large amounts of sick leave
absence on certain days particularly near weekends or after "pay day"
lateness to work in the morning or at lunch-time
leaving early
frequent absence from post whilst at work
frequent visits to cloakroom
frequent occurrences of certain illnesses
long tea or coffee breaks
high and/or increasing *incidence of accidents* both in and out of work.

Low performance standards
Missed deadlines
slow working
poor judgement
lack of attention to detail
complaints from colleagues
unreliability, forgetfulness etc.

Inter-personal problems
Unpredictable reactions to criticism
paranoia
irritability
avoiding colleagues
borrowing money
physical or verbal abuse of colleagues

In addition there are various aspects of *appearance* that should be monitored. A lack of concern for personal appearance and hygiene is often a sign that problems exist. In the case of alcohol misuse this may be accompanied by flushed face, hand tremors, general physical incapacity and the aroma of alcohol. Many people are aware of the common symptoms associated with drug misuse, such as runny nose, dilated pupils, constricted pupils etc, but it must be stressed that these are the symptoms of a number of common illnesses. Drug effects are strongly influenced by factors such as the type of drug, how much and how often, surroundings etc, so looking for common effects in individuals is a difficult task. Managers should perhaps look for evidence such as the various paraphernalia, eg syringes and spoons for drug taking, etc.

Legal aspects

The Institute would expect a common approach to employees who have alcohol or drug-related problems, that is, that the employer will act reasonably in dealing with such employees. Reasonableness is difficult to define, but Industrial Tribunals would take into account the employee's response to the problem; what facts were known to the employer at the time; whether relevant codes of practice had been followed; whether rules on alcohol and drug misuse in the workplace are clear.

Where controlled drugs are involved, another dimension is introduced by the legal aspects involved. From the employer's point of view, it is a serious offence under the Misuse of Drugs Act to allow premises to be used to produce or supply illegal drugs – it is an offence even if there is only an offer to supply drugs. For individuals it is also an offence both to possess and to supply controlled drugs.

Developing a substance-misuse policy

While it is not possible to lay down hard and fast rules for every organization, there are a number of guidelines which might be followed. An analysis of substance-misuse policies suggests that the following are the issues most likely to be covered:

1 an assurance that employees identified as having misuse problems will be offered advice and other necessary assistance

2 any absence from work necessary to receive treatment will be as granted under the organization's sickness scheme
3 an opportunity to discuss the matter once it has become evident or suspected that work performance is being affected by substance-related problems
4 the right to be accompanied at any discussion by a friend or employee representative
5 the right to full confidentiality
6 the provision of agencies to whom an employee can be referred for help *or* a commitment to provide the same expertise where employers operate their own treatment or counselling services
7 the safeguarding of all employment rights during any period of treatment, including the right to return to the same job or to suitable alternative employment
8 the links between the substance-misuse policy and the disciplinary procedure
9 the policy to deal with subsequent reversions
10 the procedure for monitoring, evaluating and reviewing the policy
11 the designation of responsibilities for ensuring that the policy is carried out and the selection of the person primarily responsible for its implementation
12 a commitment to
   (a) an employee education programme, and
   (b) a training programme for designated staff to provide them with the skills and knowledge necessary to carry out their duties under the policy

Most of these issues are straightforward; some of them, however, need clarification.

Confidentiality

Employees with substance-misuse problems who are referred for treatment, whether voluntarily or mandatorily, must be treated in confidence.

Personnel managers must accept that they may receive only the minimal information where an employee seeks help (or is referred directly) from the occupational health department or other appropriate provider of the service. This may lead to later problems, particularly if the disciplinary procedure is involved, but, by and large, employees should reasonably expect the same degree of confidentiality as from their general practitioner.

Time off, job protection etc

Many policies now treat those referred for help in the same way as for other sick leave. They are therefore entitled to receive the normal benefits under the organization's sick-pay provisions and should expect (in normal circumstances) to return to their old job with all their employment rights intact.

The role of the disciplinary procedure

The relationship between the disciplinary procedure and the substance-misuse policy is often complex. No substance-misuse policy should deny the employer the right to take disciplinary action if performance warrants it. The disciplinary procedure should normally be kept in reserve to encourage employees to accept referral and to keep them on course.

Monitoring/reviewing the policy

Initially, a policy may not be perfect, so there is always a need to monitor its operation. Keeping records allows the policy to be assessed, problems to be identified and experiences shared. Monitoring provides a valuable input to any subsequent revisions. Policies need also to keep up with the times and the growing body of knowledge about substance misuse.

If for no other reason, this makes it essential to identify an employee who has ultimate responsibility for implementing the policy.

Counselling

Counselling employees can be done in a number of ways. Some organizations do this in-house. However, it is possible, even probable, that employees seeking help with a substance-misuse problem (especially those wishing to make a voluntary referral) would prefer not to discuss the matter in-house.

Employers would be wise therefore to establish contacts with local counselling services in the fields of alcohol and drug misuse and to publish names and addresses to their workforce. Other employers have already gone further by providing a more comprehensive service through agreements with consultancies offering employee-assistance programmes. This is an issue which deserves wider attention as it would be a pity if a policy were to fail through either lack of trust or fear of dismissal holding employees back from seeking help.

Testing

Pre-employment medical tests to show up substance (particularly drug) misuse are a contentious and delicate issue. There are clearly advantages in testing: why should employers take on 'at risk' employees, especially where there are generous sick-leave benefits and/or the organization invests heavily in its pension scheme, or run the risk of its premises being used for illegal drug taking? However, there are other issues that come into the equation. First, substances can be worked out of the body in comparatively short periods. Secondly, tests may show up items such as the passive smoking of cannabis or the effects of a one-off stag night. Thirdly, unless the tests are carried out at frequent intervals, what do they prove? Finally, substance misuse is curable and, in any event, may not affect work performance.

Role and responsibilities

Every employee from the chief execuitive downwards must take on some responsibility in making the substance-misuse policy work. It is not unknown for organizations to think that putting a policy down on paper is the end of the matter. Such a statement is important, but it would be useless without a structure for implementation. There is an early need to establish what responsibilities people have at different levels in the organization. Their roles must be defined. Whilst these may vary according to the organization, the following guidelines might help:

Role of management

1 to set a good example to their subordinates and others
2 to be familiar with policy and procedures
3 to ensure that their subordinates understand the policy and their own responsibilities
4 to be alert to and to monitor changes in work performance, attendance, sickness and accident patterns
5 to take an objective and non-judgemental approach when counselling or interviewing employees
6 to refer employees for assistance when appropriate

7 to identify any aspects of the working environments which could lead to substance-abuse problems and, if possible, change them
8 to intervene early where there are signs of problems

Role of occupational health staff and employee-assistance programme

1 to provide advice and guidance on how best to help an employee who has a problem which might be related to substance misuse
2 to provide assessment of employees who refer themselves for help
3 to respond positively to referrals from managers or personnel officers
4 to provide an impartial and confidential service to employees which may include counselling, assessment and referral to another agency
5 to help identify and to assist in any education initiative to promote knowledge of alcohol and drugs.

Role of personnel function

1 at director level to have overall responsibility for implementing the policy
2 at personnel manager level to be responsible for the day to day running and co-ordination of the policy
3 at whatever level is appropriate, to refer employees for assistance, to advise on the appropriateness or otherwise of the disciplinary procedure and to ensure that personnel statistics are kept on absence and sickness levels and analysed periodically
4 to help plan and take part in providing training on substance misuse and the organization's policy
5 to follow the principles set out in this guide and ensure that they are followed by other employees.

Role of the training function
(where this differs from above)

1 to plan and provide (perhaps in conjunction with an outside agency) managers and others with training to equip them with the necessary knowledge and understanding of alcohol and drugs along with, where appropriate, basic counselling and interviewing skills

2 to increase understanding among employees about alcohol and drugs and the concepts of safe and sensible drinking
3 to inform employees in a lively and interesting way of the existence and operation of the substance-misuse policy
4 to maintain the level of internal awareness via refresher and induction packages.

Role of employee representatives
1 to take part in discussion about the substance-misuse policy
2 to help inform the workforce about the policy
3 to encourage members to seek help voluntarily
4 to advise members of their rights and responsibilities under the policy
5 to help members at work and assist with their rehabilitation
6 to encourage members to take part in appropriate education and training programmes
7 to represent members, if requested, in any problem or dispute about the application of the policy

Role of the employee
1 to find out about alcohol and drugs and the social, health and employment effects
2 to avoid covering up or colluding with colleagues
3 to urge colleagues to seek help if they have problems arising from substance misuse
4 to seek help where they themselves have problems from substance misuse
5 to be familiar with the policy and procedures
6 to use alcohol responsibly and not use illegal drugs.
(Augmented and adapted from the Health Education Authority Guidelines 1988.)

These guidelines place considerable responsibilities on managers and others, and the following issues should be borne in mind:

- many people will be dealing with substance-misuse policies for the first time in their lives
- the policy will only work if everyone involved works together
- employees may be reluctant to reveal their problems to people within the organization and/or known personally to them

- personnel and line managers should not (nor should they be expected to) diagnose illness or recommend treatment

These items lead to a series of essential steps that underpin a successful policy.

Key factors for success

Once a policy has been established, and the responsibilities apportioned, success will still hinge on a number of factors. Some of these factors apply before the policy is drawn up, others afterwards; all of them seem essential.

Consultation

The more that employees, in particular those in management, personnel and occupational health, are involved in drawing up a policy, the more they will have ownership of it and the desire to see it work. A substance-misuse policy is likely to emanate from management and will involve a great deal of management time and money; there is no reason, however, to exclude employees from the consultative process. Indeed, because of the value of guaranteeing confidentiality and the idea of peer-group pressure in substance misuse, a joint management and union/employee representative policy or monitoring committee is essential.

In some cultures, it is true, employees have not been involved at all in drawing up the substance-misuse policy – and there is no indication that the policy has suffered as a result – but by and large a policy that does have an effect on employees' private lives should be based on the broadest possible consultation.

Communication

In essence, three issues need to be communicated:

- the problems caused by substance misuse both in society and the workplace and the need, therefore, for a substance-misuse policy
- the existence and operation of the organization's policy, and
- the desirability of voluntary referral from those in need of help.

The approaches used and difficulties encountered in communicating these messages will be a function of size, number of operating units, work patterns etc. For these reasons it is as well to start the communications exercise well in advance, even before the policy is agreed. This will also raise general awareness and interest in the issue.

The usual communication methods and channels can be used. However, a large role for management, particularly line management, in briefing employees helps to get the message over and underlines management's desire to make the policy work.

Training

At the same time that the initial communications exercise takes place, organizations should be thinking about and implementing their training schedules. Line managers, who carry the brunt of operating the policy and of briefing the staff, should receive particular in-depth training.

The aim should be to ensure that at least all managers receive training in dealing with possible substance-misuse problems (although *not* diagnosing them). A high degree of awareness should be maintained through refresher courses and at induction.

Commitment

The commitment of everyone in the organization, particularly the senior management, to the policy is an essential of making the policy work.

The role of corporate culture

As with any other corporate policy, substance-misuse policies cannot be developed and implemented in a vacuum. An organization that has shown little previous interest in employee welfare matters or which has always adopted a 'management by diktat' approach to employee relations is likely to find that its substance-misuse policy is treated with suspicion. It almost certainly will not lead to voluntary referrals which should be the ultimate objective of substance-misuse policies. An open consultative style of management is more likely to generate a successful policy.

Trust is a further essential cultural influence. This trust is on a number of levels. Between manager and subordinate there must be trust:

- that confidentiality will be maintained
- that the employee realy wants to be 'cured'
- that the policy will not be abused

But it is also important that the various management groups trust each other and work well together. Line managers, in particular, must be given the maximum support and encouragement in implementing the policy. The personnel and occupational health departments must work well together.

Management must analyse the corporate culture to ensure that the policy is not undermined by environmental attitudes that support substance misuse. This means assessing the lead given by management. Some of the major questions to be considered are:

- is it necessary to serve drink in the executive dining room (or elsewhere)?
- should subsidized bars be provided?
- is drinking after working hours encouraged through peer-group pressure?
- are certain groups, by their isolation, likely to be susceptible to drinking?
- can stress, which often leads to alcohol and drug misuse, be reduced or channelled into less dangerous pursuits?

Corporate culture is an important but touchy issue. But organizations must consider whether the message they are giving via their substance-misuse policy is supported or undermined by their attitude to, in particular, alcohol in the workplace. To give two separate and incompatible messages merely confuses employees.

Finally, it goes without saying that the substance-misuse policy must relate to existing policies, that is, it should be built on and supported by policies relating to the disciplinary procedures, the sickness scheme, communication, training and welfare. This way, the substance-misuse policy will become an important and integral part of employee relations in total and in particular part of a policy of promoting good health amongst employees.

Appendix 2
Alcohol and Drugs Policy: An Example

Introduction

Alcohol and/or drug misuse can have disastrous consequences for individuals, their families and, in some circumstances, the public at large. Because it is a problem which affects a significant proportion of the population, regardless of status or occupation, it also impinges on the workplace. The evidence shows that employees who drink excessively, or inappropriately in relation to work, are more likely to have accidents at work, to be absent from work and to be less efficient than colleagues who do not do so. The same is likely to be true of employees who misuse other drugs. It is costly for both employers and employees and so the company in consultation (negotiation) with employees' representatives, has decided (agreed) to introduce an alcohol policy.

Aims of the policy

The company is concerned to provide a safe and healthy working environment. It recognizes that this can be put at risk by employees who misuse alcohol and other drugs to such an extent that it affects their health, work performance, conduct or relationships at work. This policy, which applies to all employees therefore aims to:

1 promote the health and well-being of employees and to minimize problems at work arising from alcohol and drug misuse
2 make known to employees the harmful effects of the excessive consumption of alcohol and of becoming dependent on drugs
3 encourage safe and sensible drinking habits and a drug-free life-style

4 identify employees with possible problems relating to alcohol and drug misuse at an early stage, offer guidance and actively encourage them to seek appropriate help
5 offer employees known to have alcohol or drug-related problems affecting their work referral to an appropriate agency for diagnosis and, if necessary, treatment
6 provide specific training for staff who have special responsibilities for implementing the policy

The policy does not apply to employees who commit breaches of disciplinary rules because of over-indulgence in alcohol or drugs on random occasions. While there will be an investigation of the circumstances of such offences, action may be taken under the agreed but separate disciplinary procedures.

Implementing the policy

Responsibility

The personnel director will have overall responsibility for the implementation of the alcohol and drugs policy. However, day to day responsibility will be delegated to the personnel manager who will be the designated co-ordinator of the policy. Line managers, especially first-line supervisors, will have the main responsibility for identifying employees who may be in need of help because of the effect of alcohol or drug-related problems on their work performance. They or the co-ordinator will be available at any reasonable time for confidential discussions with any employee who is concerned about his/her own drinking or experience with drugs.

Procedure

When an employee is identified as having an alcohol or drug-related problem affecting conduct at work or work performance, that employee will be asked to discuss the matter with the appropriate line manager. The line manager, while concentrating on the work situation, will inform the employee of the help available under the alcohol or drugs policy. If both parties agree, the line manager will arrange for a further interview to take place with the personnel manager. At either meeting the employee concerned will have the right to be accompanied by a friend or trade union representative.

The personnel manager will offer the employee the opportunity to seek an assessment of the problem and, if necessary, treatment from an appropriate outside agency. For this purpose, the company will establish a special relationship with a local agency. A register of other appropriate agencies will also be kept to which the employee may wish to be referred. This list will be permanently displayed on the company and trade union notice boards.

When discussing these matters the desire of the company to assist employees will at all times be uppermost in the minds of personnel and line managers. The personnel manager will make clear to an affected employee that during any period of treatment, benefits and rights laid down in the contract of employment will be safeguarded. When the employee is judged fit to resume working, it will normally be in that person's original post. If, for some reason, that is not possible, every effort will be made to find that employee suitable alternative employment in the company. Should the employee not be satisfied with the arrangements being offered, the matter may be taken up in the grievance procedure.

The procedure established by this policy for assisting an employee with an alcohol or drug-related problem is separate from the disciplinary procedure. However, where an employee with an identified alcohol or drug problem which affects conduct at work or which prevents the achievement of a satisfactory level of work performance refuses the opportunity to receive help, the matter may be referred to the agreed disciplinary procedure. Equally, where an employee denies the existence of an alcohol or drug problem or discontinues a course of treatment and then reverts to previous unsatisfactory levels of conduct or performance, the matter may be referred to the agreed disciplinary procedure.

An employee in a similar situation, who accepts the opportunity to receive help, but whose conduct or work performance afterwards reverts to the problem level, will have the new situation considered on its merits. If the personnel manager, after taking advice from the appropriate line manager, considers it justified, a further opportunity to accept help and treatment will be offered. If this course of action is not thought justified, the matter may be referred to the agreed disciplinary procedure. The employee concerned will be entitled to all the rights and safeguards laid down in the disciplinary procedure.

Confidentiality

It is recognized that certain personnel records will be necessary. However, in the case of alcohol misuse, any discussion of the nature of an employee's problems and the record of any treatment will be strictly confidential, unless the employee agrees otherwise. An agreement will be reached between the employer, the employee and the treatment agency about what can and cannot be disclosed.

In the case of drug misuse the maximum confidentiality will be preserved but it must be subject to any overriding legal requirement. Members of staff are reminded that it is unlawful for a person to be in possession of a controlled drug, except where it has been medically prescribed. It is also an offence to be in possession of a controlled drug with intent to supply it to someone else.

Staff are also informed that they may be committing a criminal offence if they knowingly allow controlled drugs to be used, kept or supplied on the company's premises. Further information and advice on this matter is available from the personnel manager.

Education and training

On commencing employment with the company every new employee will be given information about alcohol and drugs and a copy of the agreed policy. Induction training will include an explanation of the policy and an opportunity to discuss it. More specific training will be given to staff with special responsibility for implementing the policy. The areas to be covered will be determined according to the level of responsibility and the knowledge and skills considered necessary to carry out the policy successfully.

Evaluation and review

The progress of this policy will be monitored and its effect periodically evaluated. Its provisions will be reviewed from time to time in the light of such evaluation.

Appendix 3
Examples of Company Policies

An Anonymous Company

PROCEDURES FOR RECOGNITION, EVALUATION, TREATMENT AND REHABILITATION

I Recognition of Abuse

A. Company

An employee's supervisor does not have the responsibility of diagnosing substance abuse but rather to identify job performance problems which may be associated with such abuse, ie deterioration in performance, poor time-keeping, frequent sick leave. When an employee's job performance is thought to be affected by the use of substances, the supervisor should consult with his/her management and Employee Relations Department and then with the Medical Department to determine if there is sufficient evidence to warrant an evaluation. Where such evidence is apparent, the supervisor should offer the employee referral to the Medical Department for evaluation and, if indicated, assistance.

B. Employee

Employees themselves may request confidential assistance directly from the Medical Department if they have a substance abuse problem. Family or fellow employees, if they are concerned about a colleague, may consult directly with the Medical Department or one of the Department's local representatives (ie retained doctor) in the strictest confidence.

C. Medical

As the result of medical examination the Medical Department may recognise a potential or actual abuse problem.

II Evaluation

A. Supervisory Referral

An evaluation will be conducted by the Medical Department on each employee referred for assessment by his/her supervisor.

In cases where substance abuse has been confirmed and admitted, the employee and management, in consultation with the Medical Department, will agree upon a programme of treatment. The Medical Department's role will be to co-ordinate, monitor and, if necessary, participate in the treatment but *not* to provide primary patient care.

If an employee refuses to attend for evaluation or denies the existence of an obvious abuse problem, he/she will not be disciplined solely for such refusal or denial. Behaviour and performance leading to the referral will, however, be taken into account and will continue to be monitored and if unsatisfactory the employee will be subject to appropriate disciplinary procedures for these reasons.

In all cases of refusal to attend for evaluation or denial of an abuse problem, every reasonable effort will be made to persuade the employee to reconsider, emphasising that not to do so would leave the Company no other option than to act upon behaviour and/or performance.

Employees who appear to be under the influence of a substance at the time of referral will not be returned to work until completely recovered and will be subject to appropriate disciplinary action if this is confirmed.

B. Self Referral, Medical Department Recognition

In the situation where an employee is self referred or recognized by the Medical Department as having an abuse problem a similar evaluation will be conducted. Once a substance abuse problem has been confirmed, which potentially affects work, the employee will be encouraged to involve management in preparing an agreed programme of treatment. If the employee declines to involve management the Medical Department will still assist in formulating an agreed programme of treatment. (NB For reasons of medical confidentiality the Medical Department cannot inform management without the employee's consent unless there are overriding factors such as group or individual safety risks.)

III Treatment

The Company cannot undertake to provide primary medical care for its UK employees. The Medical Department's role is, together with the employee's own medical attendant, to help co-ordinate and monitor treatment and to assist directly with the situation regarding employment.

The treatment of substance abuse may involve either outpatient or inpatient care.

A. Outpatient Care

Normally outpatient care will allow the employee to continue working on a regular basis although some absence may be involved in attending for therapy, counselling etc and there may be some restriction on work activities eg travelling.

If the employee accepts his/her personal physician's recommendation for outpatient treatment an agreement will be formulated with the employee by management in consultation with the Medical Department which will contain the following commitments and any other relevant matters:

(i) The employee's line supervisor will be informed when the employee begins outpatient substance abuse treatment (Paragraph V below).

(ii) The employee will follow the treatment regimen developed by the outpatient programme and for the period specified by his/her personal physician (usually up to 24 months).

(iii) The employee will authorise the outpatient organisation to provide regular oral and written progress reports to the Medical Department on a strictly confidential basis.

(iv) The employee will report to the Medical Department during rehabilitation at the times and in the manner specified in the agreement.

(v) The employee will abstain from substance abuse as defined in the agreement.

(vi) The employee will consent to substance abuse testing by the Medical Department at any time during the treatment period.

B. Inpatient Care

If the employee accepts his/her medical attendant's recommendation for inpatient treatment an agreement will be formulated by management in consultation with the Medical Department which will contain the following commitments and any other relevant matters.

(i) The employee's line supervisor will be informed when the employee enters inpatient care for the treatment of substance abuse (Paragraph V below).

(ii) The employee will successfully complete the full inpatient programme recommended by the hospital or treatment centre. The treatment will normally be 28-45 days in length.

(iii) The employee will authorise the outpatient organisation to provide regular oral and written progress reports to the Medical Department.

C. Completion of Treatment

On completion of the inpatient treatment, an agreement will be formulated between the employee and Company management in consultation with the Medical Department which will contain the following commitments and any other relevant matters. This agreement will form the basis for the probationary period of 24 months following the employee's return to work.

(i) The employee will follow an after-care treatment programme developed co-operatively between the employee and any after-care institution for at least the minimum period recommended from the date of admission to the inpatient programme (usually up to 24 months).

(ii) The employee will authorise the treating institution to provide regular oral and written progress reports to the Medical Department.

(iii) The employee will report to the Medical Department during rehabilitation at the times and in the manner specified in the agreement.

(iv) The employee will abstain from substance abuse as defined in the agreement.

(v) The employee will consent to substance abuse testing by the Medical Department at any reasonable time during the rehabilitation period.

(vi) The employee will maintain a reasonable level of job performance, attendance and behaviour at work.

D. Refusal to Attend for Treatment

In the situation where substance abuse has been verified but treatment declined, every reasonable effort will be made to persuade the employee to reconsider, emphasising that not to do so would leave the Company no option other than to act upon the individual's behaviour and/or performance.

IV Rehabilitation Steps, Benefits and Criteria

A. Notwithstanding anything to the contrary in this Substance Abuse Policy and Procedures Guide, management retains the right at all times to discipline any employee under the following circumstances:

1. If an employee uses, sells, or possesses illegal drugs or drug paraphernalia, or consumes, sells, or possesses alcohol without prior authorisation on Company premises, the employee is subject to discipline including immediate termination and, as appropriate, notification of law enforcement authorities.
2. If the employee uses, sells, or possesses any substance, on or off Company premises, in such a way as to impair job performance or the ability to represent the Company in an appropriate manner, the employee is subject to discipline including termination.
3. If the employee's job performance deteriorates during or after treatment (ie during probation) the fact that the employee was involved in treatment will not automatically preclude the application of appropriate disciplinary procedures up to and including termination.

B. If an employee has had no prior substance abuse treatment and voluntarily requests help for a drug or alcohol problem or is recognised by the Medical Department as having one, assistance should be offered before job performance is adversely affected as described in Section II. If the management involvement is agreed, the employee should not be placed on probation unless performance deteriorates after the self-referral. An employee's request for assistance shall not affect management's right to administer appropriate disciplinary action for incidents occurring before or after the request.

C. The employee should be placed on probation if performance has deteriorated regardless of the source of referral. The probation should continue during and following the treatment period until performance has been satisfactory for a reasonable period of time as determined by management. Management should offer assistance as described in *Procedures,* Section III.

D. The rehabilitation programme will generally cover a treatment period of 24 months. The type of assistance can be *either* outpatient or inpatient as previously described.

1. *Outpatient Treatment*
The employee remains on the job and actively participates in an outpatient treatment programme (NB the job duties may have been modified or changed after consultation with the Medical Department). The treatment programme is usually phased, the first consisting normally of intensive therapy and the second of regular (ie weekly) meetings.
Time off work is allowed so that the employee may attend the programme. Absences of whole days are recorded for the purposes of the Statutory Sick Pay Regulations using normal Company self-certification procedures.

2. *Inpatient Treatment*
If the employee enters a substance abuse treatment programme on an inpatient basis:
(i) The employee will receive pay, in accordance with the provisions of the appropriate sickness absence policy, during the period of absence from work.

(ii) Following discharge and return to work, absences for follow-up treatment and rehabilitation will be dealt with as in outpatient treatment above.

E. If, after the job performance having returned to a satisfactory level through rehabilitation outlined under IV D above, the employee in the opinion of the Company has a recurring substance abuse problem and job performance is again affected, *one* of the following courses of action should be taken so long as appropriate disciplinary action (eg termination) does not preclude them.

1. The employee should be placed on rehabilitative leave up to a maximum of 90 days without pay which will be authorised in accordance with the appropriate authority limitations. During this period:
   (a) No wages, bonus, or other forms of compensation will be paid.
   (b) Employees will not be eligible to continue, through direct remittance, Stock Ownership Plan, AVCs etc.
   (c) Coverage for Accidental Death and Dismemberment, Group Term Life Insurance, and the Whole Life Insurance will continue.
   (d) In the case of an employee being provided with a Company-owned car, he/she will no longer be permitted to drive it. Permission for the employee's spouse only to drive the vehicle can be approved by management.
   (e) Creditable service will be allowed for Pension Plan, and safety and service awards will also continue to accrue.
   (f) An employee's next year holiday entitlement will be reduced by 1/12 for each 30 calendar days the employee is on leave.
   (g) The employee must seek rehabilitation and contact the Medical Department by phone or in person at least twice monthly so that rehabilitation progress can be evaluated.
   (h) The employee will authorise his or her personal medical attendant to provide regular oral or written progress reports to the Medical Department.

If the offer of leave is refused, the employee will be terminated in accordance with recognised procedures.

Following the rehabilitative leave *either* the employee may return to work if in the opinion of the Medical Department and the appropriate member of management, in accordance with authority limitations, the employee is able to perform his/her duties satisfactorily. The employee should be placed on probation for an additional 24 months following his/her return to work.

Or if the employee fails to achieve successful rehabilitation during that period, the employee's contract of employment will be terminated in accord with recognised procedures.

2. Management may, with support from the Medical Department, consider a second treatment programme outlined under Section III above. This action would be considered only under unusual circumstances and solely at management's discretion and requires the approval of a Chairman and Managing Director.
   (a) The employee must have demonstrated sustained satisfactory job performance and a lengthy substance-free period (at least one year from the end of the first treatment period).
   (b) The employee will be placed on probation for the second treatment period.
   (c) Following this treatment, the employee may return to work only if, in the opinion of management and the Medical Department, the employee is rehabilitated and able to do a satisfactory job. Otherwise, the employee's service should be terminated.

3. No more than two treatment programmes should be authorised for the treatment of any combination of drug or alcohol abuse.

F. If job performance does not improve under C following the initial treatment period, the employee should be placed on rehabilitative leave without pay for 90 days or be terminated.

G. If job performance is affected and there is reason to believe substance abuse may be the cause, an employee is subject to discipline for failure to co-operate in this Substance Abuse Programme in the following circumstances:

1. The employee refuses or fails to report to the Medical Department for evaluation for suspected substance abuse.
2. The employee refuses or fails to attend for treatment after confirmation of substance abuse.
3. The employee refuses to co-operate in treatment for substance abuse.

V Medical Confidentiality

The Medical Division will retain information on an employee evaluated or treated for substance abuse in the same confidential manner as it keeps all other medical records. With the employee's permission, his/her supervisor will be informed when an employee has begun inpatient or outpatient substance abuse treatment and with the employee's permission the Medical Department will report to management on employee's progress during treatment and rehabilitation. Such disclosures will be on a strict need to know basis to preserve confidentiality.

VI Personnel Records

The supervisor must maintain pertinent accurate and detailed records of all matters associated with performance, safety, discipline, especially if these are thought to be connected with substance abuse. These records will include instances of unsatisfactory work performance, conferences with the employee, dates of consultations with the Medical Department, referral to the Medical Department, reasons for disciplinary actions, warnings given to the employee, and the like. Such records should contain detailed observations of the employee's physical appearance and behaviour, where appropriate, and should be dated and signed by the supervisor. All records must be maintained in a secure location to protect confidentiality.

VII Transportation for Employees Sent Home and Incapable of Driving

When an employee appears to be impaired by the improper use of substances, the employee should be sent home. The Supervisor should insist that the employee not drive a vehicle and to that end, the supervisor should do the following:

A. If the employee drives a Company vehicle, permission to do so must be withdrawn immediately.

B. Arrange transportation through a friend or relative of the employee or through a transportation service.

C. If suitable transportation cannot be arranged and the employee is manageable, allow the employee to remain on company premises in a restricted area until transportation is available or the employee is no longer impaired.

D. If the employee refuses the above or is unmanageable, appropriate assistance should be summoned. The individual cannot be physically restrained from leaving the premises but the Company reserves the right to protect third parties and property and will notify law enforcement agencies if circumstances warrant.

VIII Awareness

To ensure that employees, visitors, and contractors and their employees are aware of the company's policy prohibiting the possession or use of alcoholic beverages (unless authorised), illegal drugs, and drug paraphernalia on Company premises, and the Company's right to search personnel and personal effects, signs could be posted at all gates or other entry points or in visitors' signature books.

PROCEDURE FOR ACUTE SITUATIONS

A. Company Employees

Should a supervisor or manager either suspect or observe that an employee is using drugs or drinking alcohol on the job or is creating an immediate and obvious disruption or potential safety situation with the appearance of alcohol or drug influence the following procedures should be followed if possible:

1. Since it is useful to have a witness to events, call for assistance, eg another supervisor, Security or ER personnel.
2. If possible with the consent and co-operation of the employee involved:
   (a) Secure any evidence (eg alcohol container, drugs, paraphernalia etc) and seal it in an envelope or other container, signing and dating the same.
   (b) Remove employee into an office or quiet location.
3. Preferably with a witness present confront the employee with the observed actions or symptoms and ask for an explanation (NB No attempt at diagnosis should be made nor must the individual be accused of being intoxicated etc; describe only actions or behaviour observed.)
4. If there is a medical department at the location take the employee there; if there is none or it is closed, follow the procedures which have been laid down for obtaining medical assistance.

   If it is thought the individual is seriously ill, or in need of urgent medical attention, transport to a local hospital should be arranged.
5. On completion of investigations the employee should be suspended from duties until further notice.
6. When fit to do so, the employee is then to be sent home by the most convenient method except by the individual driving him or herself. If the employee becomes belligerent and refuses to leave or insists on driving, site security should take appropriate action (see Paragraph VII above).

7. As soon as possible complete a report documenting all observations, responses from employees and actions taken.
8. Review problem with Employee Relations and follow normal disciplinary procedure.
9. An uncooperative or belligerent employee presents a potentially difficult problem. Appropriate steps should be taken to ensure the safety of the individual involved, third parties and company property including the involvement of security, medical and ER departments. It is particularly important to document events as disciplinary action will result.

B. Non-Company Personnel

1. Call for assistance (eg another supervisor, Security or Employee Relations personnel) and, if available, a representative of the individual's own employing organization.

   Follow steps 2, 3, 4, 5, 6, 7 and 9 as detailed for Company employees with the exception that in paragraph 6 the individual's employing organization if possible should be responsible for the logistical arrangements.
2. In such situations the individual involved will probably be excluded from Company premises in future.

Aer Lingus

Policy

It is the airlines policy:

1.1 To treat with understanding employees suffering from alcoholism and/or drug addiction and their related illnesses in the same way as employees having other illnesses.

1.2 To ensure that they will not encounter prejudice in relation to job security or promotional prospects provided that they achieve and maintain the capabilities, competence and qualifications necessary for performing their work.

1.3 To provide them with the normal sickness privileges throughout the treatment phase of rehabilitation.

1.4 To take appropriate steps to raise the level of staff awareness about alcoholism, drug addiction and their related illnesses with the purpose of eliminating the social stigma and encouraging people to come forward voluntarily for help.

1.5 To make this help readily available to those seeking it.

Alcoholism

2.1 The airline subscribes to the medical opinion that excessive drinking can lead to chronic progressive alcohol-related illnesses and to alcoholism which if untreated can result in permanent disability or death. It is also recognized that it is an illness for which treatment and rehabilitation can be successful, given the full co-operation of the individual.

2.2 For the purpose of this policy, alcoholism is defined as a condition in which a person's consumption of any alcoholic beverage definitely and repeatedly interferes with that person's health and/or job performance.

Social Drinking

3. This policy is not concerned with social drinking but with alcoholism. The primary concern is the effect of uncontrolled drinking on the individual's job performance and health, but it is recognized that such behaviour will have detrimental effects on home family life.

Objective

4. The policy is designed solely to achieve restoration of health and full recovery.

Responsibility

5. The decision to request diagnosis and to accept treatment for alcoholism is the personal responsibility of the individual.

Early Identification and Help

6.1 The effectiveness of this policy in achieving recovery depends to a great extent on early identification of the problem and professional care. The help of colleagues, shop stewards and supervisors can play a vital role in encouraging the person to seek help at an early stage when the chances of recovery are greatest.

6.2 Where a deterioration in job performance, behaviour or attitude may be caused by a drink problem, an individual will be encouraged to seek counselling and appropriate treatment.

Refusal to Accept Help

7. An individual's refusal to accept referral for diagnosis or to follow prescribed treatment will be handled in accordance with normal practice covering unsatisfactory work performance, if appropriate.

Confidentiality

8. All Medical records and referral for treatment will be treated with the same confidentiality as applies to other illnesses.

Drug Problems

9. As indicated in paragraph 1 above, this policy will also apply to employees with other drug-related problems.

Management's Responsibility

10. Nothing in this statement of policy is to be interpreted as constituting a waiver of management's responsibility, exercised through the supervisory chain to maintain discipline or its right to take disciplinary measures for the reasons and in accordance with the procedure agreed with the appropriate trade union on conduct and disciplinary procedures.

Birmingham City Council

1. Introduction

1.1 The City Council recognises that there is a significant number of employees whose consumption of alcohol may bring harm to their own lives and possibly their families, friends and others. This harm will be reflected in reduced levels of performance at work together with increased absenteeism and sickness.

1.2 This policy has been developed and introduced by the City Council with the aim of helping any employee who has a problem with the consumption of alcohol to overcome it. The policy has been agreed with the City's recognised trade unions and it applies to all employees. However, before help can be given effectively an employee must accept that an alcohol problem exists.

2. Scope and Definitions

2.1 This policy encompasses any use of or consumption of alcohol which is habitual and adversely affects an employee's work performance, safety, health or welfare at work. Excessive regular consumption of alcohol may well lead to dependence and danger to health in the long term.

2.2 The policy recognises that where an employee has an alcohol related problem, this will be regarded for employment purposes as an illness. This does not preclude normal use of the disciplinary procedure when an employee is under the influence of alcohol or other substances and behaves in a manner contrary to the standards of safety and behaviour required by the City Council of its employees.

2.3 Thus, absence whilst receiving medical or other recognized treatment will be treated as sick leave and normally will not affect any other condition of employment. The duration of the period for which support is offered should normally relate to the progress made by the employee in overcoming the problem and the ability of management to maintain the level of support being offered. The fact that an employee seeks help together with any associated information or records will be kept completely confidential to the recognized individuals and/or agencies within the procedure designated by this policy.

2.4 Every encouragement will be given to employees to seek appropriate help. Supervisors and managers have the most important role to play in identifying problems at work. They are the most likely to observe unsatisfactory behaviour and raise the matter with the employee as part of normal supervision with the aim of preventing further occurrence. In this process supervisors should be alert to the possibility of an alcohol problem. Guidelines will be issued to help supervisors to do this.

3. The Procedure

3.1 It is important to the success of the policy that supervisors play an active role and are encouraged to consult Departmental Personnel Officers before approaching employees concerned. Supervisors who believe an employee to have a problem with drink should advise the employee and explain the help that is available under the policy. Their aim should be to refer the employee to the Occupational Health Service. They are not required to discuss the personal aspects of alcohol related problems in any detail. If, in these circumstances, a supervisor needs to raise an issue about work performance or behaviour and the employee concerned is unable to give a satisfactory explanation, the supervisor should indicate his/her suspicions about a possible drink problem. It should then be explained that help can be given provided that the employee will accept that an alcohol problem exists.

3.2 At all stages of the referral process confidentiality must be maintained. Any employee is free to approach the Occupational Health Service directly and in these cases, confidentiality will be respected, but individuals will be encouraged to allow their Departmental Personnel Officers and, ideally, their line managers to be informed.

3.3 If the employee refuses help or fails to co-operate fully with counselling or treatment and work problems continue, then the disciplinary procedure applies as normal, but action should only be taken after advice has been sought from the Occupational Health Service. This needs to be done to exclude other medical problems as a cause of poor work performance, eg anxiety, stress, etc.

4. Sources of Assistance

4.1 The focus of assistance will be the Occupational Health Service who will diagnose the extent of the problem, give help directly or refer the employee to a recognized external agency. Treatment will be monitored by the OHS and the Personnel Officer of the Department concerned who will be kept informed in general terms of overall progress.

4.2 The employee may approach the Departmental Personnel Officer in the first instance, who may be able to hold an initial discussion but should refer the case for expert diagnosis to the OHS. Departmental Personnel Officers will be required to keep themselves informed about individual cases and advise supervisors on measures to be taken in the workplace as a consequence, as well as welfare advice that may be appropriate.

5. Training and Guidance

5.1 The members of the OHS will be given supplementary training in monitoring this condition in employees as well as diagnosing the extent of the problem, making referrals and the general management of cases involving habitual consumption of alcohol.

5.2 Departmental Personnel Officers will need to receive general training in the nature of alcohol problems, their identification, talking to people who have such problems and the general nature of treatments that can be obtained. The aim of this training will be to give a general understanding of the subject and to be able to encourage and give informed advice to employees volunteering or supervisors who feel they have a problem to deal with.

5.3 Seminars of a general nature should be arranged for other personnel employees, Safety Officers and others for whom it would be relevant.

5.4 Guidelines will be issued to supervisors, who will also, where appropriate, attend briefing sessions arranged by personnel officers. The Director of Personnel and Equal Opportunities will prepare training materials for use in departments and will offer instruction in their use. Individuals may sometimes approach a trade union representative in the first instance and this possibility has been accepted by the recognized trade unions. Guidance notes will be made available to trade unions accordingly. Trade unions should be encouraged to use the Occupational Health Service.

6. Making the Policy Known

6.1 This policy will be made known to all employees by means of noticeboards and circulars. Colleagues of people known or thought to have a problem with drink will be encouraged to draw their attention to the policy.

6.2 As part of a continuing health education programme, posters or other materials will be circulated from time to time to remind people of the help that is available, together with information about the potential harm from habitual consumption of alcohol. It will be emphasised in the educational material that the policy applies to *all* employees. For example, the point will be made that the safe levels of alcohol consumption for women is less than for men.

6.3 This material will be produced by the Department of Personnel and Equal Opportunities and made available to personnel officers in departments for circulation as appropriate to each department.

7. Reviews

7.1 The operation of this policy will be reviewed by the Personnel and Equal Opportunities Committee in consultation with the appropriate trade unions.

Marconi Command and Control Systems Ltd

Procedures

1. The decision to drink alcoholic beverages is a personal matter which does not concern the Company. The Company is concerned with employees' drinking habits only in so far as these have a detrimental effect on job performance and safety.
2. Employees with drinking problems are encouraged to seek help voluntarily and before their job performance is affected by contacting either the Co-ordinator for the Alcohol Advisory Service at Rugby or the local Co-ordinator at Frimley. Any decision on the part of the employees to seek help will not interfere with their employment. Confidentiality will be maintained at all times.
3. Unsatisfactory job performance in which alcohol abuse is suspected to be a factor will be the grounds for mandatory referral to the Co-ordinator, Alcohol Advisory Service for assessment. The employee will be interviewed and advised of the referral and if they so wish, will have the right to be accompanied by a union representative at the interview.
4. The decision to accept advice and treatment for problem drinking is the personal responsibility of the individual employee. The employee, however, remains responsible for his or her own work record and continued unsatisfactory job performance will result in appropriate disciplinary action up to and including dismissal.
5. Employees who volunteer or are mandatorily referred for assessment, and who decide to accept treatment, will be entitled to sick leave subject to the normal conditions. Full confidentiality will be maintained at all times.
6. In cases of mandatory referral, every effort will be made to ensure that the employee retains his/her present job with no long term detriment to his/her promotion opportunities or other benefits, so long as his/her work performance returns to an acceptable level.
7. Where an employee is incapable of retaining his/her present job, or where doing so would present a serious safety hazard

to himself/herself or others, or would be an impediment to his/her own recovery, every effort will be made to find alternative employment within the Company.

8. Assistance under the programme does not permit an employee to abuse normal responsibilities of employment. Existing regulations with respect to intoxication or drinking on the site will continue to be enforced, ie it is an offence to bring or partake of alcohol on any Company site.
9. Nothing in this Code of Practice is to be interpreted as constituting a waiver of management responsibility to maintain discipline, or the right to take disciplinary action within the framework of existing agreements.
10. Assistance under this programme does not prevent recourse to normal Grievance or Disciplinary procedures.

The Role of Management

To provide through education a general climate of awareness of the manifestations and dangers of excessive and inappropriate consumption of alcohol for occupational health and safety.

Also through education to help the workforce, as a whole, understand the rationale of the policy on problem drinking and the associated procedures.

To facilitate the training of supervisory and other staff in order to be able to implement the policy.

To establish clear lines of responsibility and case handling procedures.

To reassess periodically the effectiveness of the programme.

Appendix 4
Case Studies

Case Study (A)

Jack Jones is a supervisor who has worked for the company for twenty years. His wife died recently; they had been very close. Jack has a son and daughter, both married. The son lives in the North of England but the daughter lives quite near. They are not ones for visiting each other very much.

Generally speaking, Jack Jones is a good supervisor but there are times when he is very aggressive toward the people for whom he is responsible. Most people like Jack but when he has these bouts of aggression he seems to be a changed person and not very likeable at all.

Recently, this kind of behaviour has been increasing and causing discontent among his work group. At times Jack's behaviour affects the group's work performance. It has also been upsetting his supervisory colleagues.

No one has made an official complaint about Jack's behaviour but there are whispers that something should be done about it. The whispers have come to the attention of Jack's own line manager, Jim Johnson. It occurred to him that there have been times when he thought he had caught a whiff of drink on Jack's breath.

How should the following deal with the situation

the employees in Jack's work group?

Jack's fellow supervisors?

Jack's manager, Jim Johnson?

Case Study (B)

Fred Smith is employed as a crane driver and has been employed with the company for three years. It is known that he has been experiencing domestic difficulties and his marriage is in a very shaky state. Fred is a shift worker and he has been allowed time and changes of shift to deal with his home situation.

On a number of occasions he has come on night duty smelling of drink. On one occasion he was found asleep in the mess room when he should have returned to the job after an official break. No action had been taken against Fred but his supervisor told him to pull himself together.

On a later occasion, again on night shift, he was seen drinking in the mess room. This led to a general warning being given to staff about drinking at work but Fred Smith was not given a specific warning about his conduct. Three weeks later he was involved in an accident with his crane. No one was hurt but it could have been very serious. When the supervisor questioned him about the circumstances of this accident Fred was again smelling of drink.

What should be done about Fred Smith by

management?

trade union representative?

Case Study (C)

Frances Wright is a clerk in a busy office of about thirty men and women. The work she does is fairly routine but needs to be kept up to date as otherwise it causes difficulties for others in the office. Frances's work also includes filing. She has worked for the company for seven years since leaving school at 16.

Frances is a bright woman who gained five O Levels before leaving school. Lately, however, her work has become slipshod and often records cannot be found in her files. On a number of occasions she has been away from work on Mondays. Each time her mother telephones the office to say Frances is not well. Two or three times a week she goes off on her own at lunch-time and comes back to work late, usually in a rather obstreperous mood.

Frances is popular with everyone in the office because of her normally friendly disposition. Nevertheless, because she seems to be getting away with her slap-happy approach to work, some of her colleagues are beginning to get a bit fed up with Frances.

Not much is known about Frances's private life. In spite of her rather extroverted behaviour during working hours she does not mix socially with her office colleagues after work. This has been regarded as rather odd but not taken too much amiss.

1. Do you think that Frances might have problems?

2. How should Frances's colleagues in the office deal with the situation?

3. What should management do?

4. If it turns out that Frances has a drink problem, what kind of help might be available to her?

Case Study (D)

David Hughes is thirty-five years of age and married with one son. He is the deputy chief engineer in a company employing several hundred engineers working on various aspects of design and development research. Unlike most of his senior colleagues, who are university educated, David has made his way through practical experience and part-time study.

David has been deputy chief engineer for eighteen months since being selected by a firm of management consultants on behalf of the company. To take up his new post he had left an aircraft company in the West of England where he had established a reputation as a hard-working, innovative engineer. Neither David nor his family has found the move from the West to the Southeast of England easy, but he wants to make a go of it.

David was recruited as the intended replacement of the chief engineer who will retire in six months' time. When David takes over as chief engineer he will have direct management responsibility for all engineering staff. He will be expected not only to judge the ideas and work of other well-qualified and experienced people but also be a source of inspiration and new ideas. To prepare him for the succession the company has spent a considerable amount of money on putting David through various courses at prestigious university business schools.

Lately, the chief engineer has begun to wonder if David is the right person to succeed him. He has no doubt about his ability but he does seem to be under a constant strain. Not only that, David has made a nuisance of himself on more than one occasion at social and business functions. On these occasions he has drunk more than was good for him or the company. There have also been times at work when a senior management team has been grappling with serious problems and David does not seem to have been quite with it. At these times he has not made the kind of contribution expected of someone in his position. A colleague mentioned this to him on one occasion and he became quite angry and agitated.

1. What do you think David's problem might be?
2. What would be the best way of handling the situation?
3. What kind of considerations should management have in mind?

Case Study (E)

Jane Brown is a regional personnel manager in a major bank. She has held the post for about three months. Peter Walker, a regional manager, reports to her that one of his managers, Ken Jones, has been disciplined for not maintaining his bank account in a proper fashion. The first stage of the procedure had resulted in a warning being given that if the account was not properly maintained in future further action would be taken and dismissal could result. In spite of this the account was once again out of order and Jane Brown was told by the senior manager that he has no alternative but to take further disciplinary action.

The senior manager believes that the problem has been caused by Ken Jones' excessively hospitable attitude. He is a very sociable individual who is always first to the bar and enjoys the company of friends and colleagues at the local pub and sports club. Peter Walker admits to the personnel manager that Ken Jones' lunch hours have been getting longer and, although he is sometimes involved in entertaining customers, more often than not he visits the local pub with colleagues. In response to questioning the senior manager admits that probably the quality and quantity of the manager's work is reduced in the afternoons.

The personnel manager, Jane Brown, asks the senior manager to look into the manager's account difficulties and ascertain why he is taking unauthorized overdrafts. It becomes clear that, not only are many cheques being cashed at the local pub, but also, when a loan was granted at the time of the first-stage disciplinary action being taken, a cheque for £800 was issued to the same public house indicating that a debt could have been accumulated there.

On reading the file note of the disciplinary interview, the personnel manager finds that when the manager was asked why he was having financial problems the manager did say that he thought he drank a bit too much and that 'booze' was expensive these days. There was no further reference to drink or drink-related problems in the manager's personnel file.

Subsequently, the personnel manager speaks to the senior manager and agrees with him that if indeed all the money being cashed at the pub is being spent on drink then the manager must be consuming a lot of alcohol. Since the first meeting between the senior manager and the personnel manager the former has looked at some of the files maintained by the manager and has found several errors. There has been a noticeable deterioration in the work being done. The records also indicate an increase in the manager's absence due to sickness. As an aside the senior manager tells the personnel manager that a colleague has been talking to the manager's wife who had moaned about the long hours her husband was having to work. She complained that he was late home every night. In fact the manager was seen to leave the office every evening promptly at 5.30pm.

What should the personnel manager do?

Appendix 5
Guide to Drug Types

The following will provide a brief outline of the different categories of drugs and the effects they can have on the system. For a more in-depth description please refer to *Drug Misuse – A Basic Briefing* (ISDD, 1985), available free from the Institute for the Study of Drug Dependence.

Opiates: heroin, morphine, methadone

Effects
Opiates are designed to dull pain. In medicine they are used in the management of serious burns and in the control of pain in the terminally ill. They create a sense of euphoria, suppress coughing, cause constipation.

Long-term effects
Physical dependency, and/or psychological dependency. Withdrawal symptoms will occur, once tolerance has developed, between 8 and 24 hours after last administration. The withdrawal effects include tremor, aches and pains in joints and limbs and sweating. There are many more symptoms which may occur. The withdrawal symptoms vary from person to person in both intensity and type.

Stimulants: cocaine, amphetamine (speed), caffeine

Effects
Increases heart rate and breathing, decreases appetite. Users report feeling more confident and cheerful.

Long-term effects
Audio and visual distortion, weight loss, paranoia. Heart failure has been reported in a few people. Because stimulants suppress appetite and increase the body's normal rate of functioning, hunger and fatigue occur when the person stops taking the drug.

Hallucinogens: LSD, 'magic mushrooms' etc.

Effects

Hallucinogens produce changes in the body's sensory perceptions: the senses become far more acute. The overall effect is to alter the user's perception of reality. This can sometimes produce feelings of paranoia, if the person is in a depressed state of mind whilst under the influence of the drug.

Long-term effects

A tolerance can build up requiring more of the drug in order to obtain the desired effect. This is uncommon as people tend to use the drug on a casual basis. Flashbacks to the actual experience of the drug may occur. For some people this can be extremely distressing, causing some doubt as to their sanity. The flashbacks do recede in time.

Sedatives – barbiturates: Tuinal, Seconal etc.

Effects

They calm the individual, in much the same way as alcohol would, if taken in small doses. They offer relaxation and a release from anxiety. Taking them in larger doses, the user becomes clumsy and loses control of movement and speech, often appearing to be drunk.

Long-term effects

Tolerance builds up, requiring more of the drug to obtain the original effect. Physical and psychological dependence occurs leading to a withdrawal syndrome. The syndrome includes irritability, nausea, delirium. If the person stops using the drug suddenly, he/she may suffer from blackouts, which in some cases may be fatal.

Tranquillizers

Effects

Used primarily to induce sleep. These are not as popular with illegal drug users. If mixed with alcohol the effect is heightened, as with many drugs. This may lead to overdose.

Long-term effects

A tolerance develops as does a physical and psychological dependence. The withdrawal syndrome is similar to that of barbiturates. It may take a long time for the syndrome to be completed.

Cannabis

Effects

The effects of the drug are dependent on the individual's state of mind at the time of use. The overall effect is to heighten feelings and emotions. The individual may become happier or more depressed as a result. The user will find manual tasks more difficult whilst under the influence of cannabis although this varies from person to person.

Long-term effects

There is no conclusive evidence to suggest that cannabis causes any physical damage. As with any drug, one can become psychologically dependent.

Appendix 6
Organizations dealing with Alcohol and Drug Misuse

National Organizations

England and Wales

Alcohol Concern
305 Grays Inn Road, London WC1X 8QF
01-833 3471

Health Education Authority
78 New Oxford Street, London WC1A 1AH
01-631 0930

Institute of Alcohol Studies
Alliance House, Caxton Street, London
SW1M 0QS 01-222 5880

Standing Conference on Drug Abuse
1-4 Hatton Place, Hatton Garden, London
EC1N 8ND 01-831 3595
The national co-ordinating body for voluntary organizations and agencies.

Drugs, Alcohol, Women Nationally
Boundary House, 91-92 Charterhouse Street,
London EC1M 6HR 01-250 3284

The Institute for the Study of Drug Dependence
1/4 Hatton Place, Hatton Garden, London
EC1N 8ND 01-430 1991
A library, information and research resource on all aspects of drug use and misuse.

Release
169 Commercial Street, London E1 3BW
01-377 5905
A legal service on drug-related problems.

Scotland

Scottish Council on Alcohol
147 Blythswood Street, Glasgow G2 4EN
041-333 9677

Scottish Health Education Group
Woodburn House, Canaan Lane, Edinburgh
EH10 4SG 031-447 8044

Northern Ireland

Northern Ireland Council on Alcohol
40 Elmswood Avenue, Belfast BT9 6AZ
0232 664434

Ireland

Irish National Council for Alcoholism
19 Fleet Street, Dublin 2
774832

Rutland Centre Ltd
Knocklyon House, Knocklyon Road,
Dublin 16 946358

Alcoholism Counselling Service
Stanhope Street, Dublin 7
779447

St Patrick's Hospital Psychiatric Service
James Street, Dublin 8
710297

Alcoholics Anonymous
109 South Circular Road, Dublin 8
795967

St John of God Hospital
Stillorgain, County Dublin
881781

Organizations with Local Groups/Projects

Turning Point
CAP House, 9/12 Long Lane, London
EC1A 9HA 01-606 3947

Aquarius
3rd Floor, The White House, 111 New Street,
Birmingham B2 4EU
021-632 4727

Appendix 7
References

Chapter 1

ALCOHOL CONCERN. *The Drinking Revolution*. London, 1987.
ALCOHOL CONCERN. *Factsheet*. London, 1988.
McDONNELL R. and MAYNARD A. 'The Costs of Alcohol Misuse'. *British Journal of Addiction*. 80, 1985, pp27-35.
CENTRAL STATISTICAL OFFICE. *Annual Abstract of Statistics*. London, HMSO, 1988.
OFFICE OF POPULATION CENSUSES AND SURVEYS. *Population Trends* 7. London, HMSO, Spring 1977.
THE BREWERS' SOCIETY. *Statistical Handbook*. London, 1986.
CENTRAL POLICY REVIEW STAFF. *Alcohol Policies*. Stockholm, Socioligska Institutionen, 1979.
KREITMAN N. 'Alcohol Consumption and the Preventive Paradox'. *British Journal of Addiction,* 81, 1986, pp353-63.
DIGHT, S.E. *Scottish Drinking Habits*. London, HMSO, 1976.
BREEZE E. *Women and Drinking*. London, HMSO, 1985.

Chapter 2

EDWARDS G. *et al.* 'Clients of Alcohol Information Centres'. *British Medical Journal*. 4, 1967, pp346-9.
KENYON W.H. and GRANT M. *eds. Alcoholism and Industry,* Liverpool, AEC and Merseyside, Lancashire and Cheshire Council on Alcoholism, 1977, pp46-51.
KREITMAN N. 'Alcohol Consumption and the Preventive Paradox'. *British Journal of Addiction*. 81, 1986, pp353-63.
LATCHAM R.W. *et al.* 'Regional Variations in British Alcohol Morbidity Rates: A Myth Uncovered?' *British Medical Journal*. 289, 1984, pp1341-5.
BEAUMONT P.B. and ALLSOP S.J. 'Beverage Report'. *Occupational Safety and Work*. Vol.13, No.10, October 1983, pp25-9.
WILSON P. *Drinking in England and Wales*. London, HMSO, 1980.
STEVENSON R.W. 'Absenteeism in an industrial plant due to alcoholism'. *Quarterly Journal of Studies on Alcohol,* 1942. Quoted in HORE B. and PLANT M.A. *eds. Alcohol Problems in Employment*. London, Croom Helm, 1981.
SAAD E.S.M. and MADDEN J.S. 'Certificated Incapacity and Unemployment in Alcoholics'. *British Journal of Psychiatry*. 128, 1976, pp340-5.
HOLTERMANN S. and BURCHELL A. *Government Economic Service Working Paper,* London, DHSS, 1981.
CENTRAL STATISTICAL OFFICE. *Social Trends*. London, HMSO, 1986.
PLANT M.A. *Drugs in Perspective*. London, Hodder and Stoughton, 1987.
LABOUR RESEARCH DEPARTMENT. *Bargaining Report*. London, 1986.
McDONNELL R. and MAYNARD A. 'The Costs of Alcohol Misuse'. *British Journal of Addiction*. 80, 1985, pp27-35.
ALCOHOL CONCERN. *The Drinking Revolution*. London, 1987.
CONFEDERATION OF BRITISH INDUSTRY/TURNING POINT. *Danger: Drugs at Work*. London, 1986.

Chapter 3

THE HEALTH AND SAFETY EXECUTIVE. *The Problem Drinker at Work.* London, HMSO, 1981. (Occasional Paper Series, OP1.)
KREITMAN N. 'Alcohol Consumption and the Preventive Paradox'. *British Journal of Addiction.* 81, 1986, pp353-63.
LATCHAM R.W. *et al.* 'Regional Variations . . .'. *British Medical Journal.* 289, 1984, pp1341-5.
INTERNATIONAL LABOUR ORGANIZATION. *Responses to Alcohol and Drug Abuse in the Workplace.* Geneva, 1987.
THE BREWERS' SOCIETY. *Statistical Handbook.* London, 1986.
LABOUR RESEARCH DEPARTMENT. *Bargaining Report.* London, 1986.
THE HEALTH EDUCATION AUTHORITY in association with Alcohol Concern and the National Health Service Training Authority. *Guidelines for Health Authorities on the Development, Implementation and Evaluation of an Alcohol Policy for their Staff.* London, 1988.

Chapter 4

TETHER P. and ROBINSON D. 'Alcohol and Work: "Policies" are not enough'. *Alcohol and Alcoholism,* 20, 1985, pp1-3.
HEALTH EDUCATION AUTHORITY. *Guidelines for Health Authorities.* London, 1988.

Chapter 5

THE HEALTH AND SAFETY EXECUTIVE. *The Problem Drinker at Work.* London, HMSO, 1981. (Occasional Paper Series, OP1.)
LUCAS E.G. 'Alcohol in Industry'. *British Medical Journal.* 294, 1987, pp460-61, citing HYMAN J. and BEAUMONT P.B. 'Identifying the Problem Drinker'. *Occupational Safety and Health.* 14, 1984, pp24-9.
KENYON W.H. 'Company Policies and Programmes', in KENYON W.H. and GRANT M. *eds. Alcohol and Industry* (above).
MAYNARD A. 'Alcohol Use: Costs and benefits'. *Alcohol Concern.* Vol.1, No.2, 1985, pp11-12.
EMERY M. 'Alcohol and Safety in Industry'. *Journal of Social and Occupational Medicine.* 36, 1986, pp18-23.
British Leyland v Swift (1981) IRLR 91.
Davis v Atkins (1977) AC 931.
Polkey v A.E.Dayton Services HL (1987) 3 AER 974.
Post Office v Fennell (1981) IRLR 221.
Spence v Paragon Wallpapers (1977) ICR 301.
British Home Stores v Burchell (1978) IRLR 379.
Roberts v Toyota (GB) Ltd (1980) SCOIT S/2821/80.
DEPARTMENT OF EMPLOYMENT. *Code of Practice on Disciplinary Procedures.* London, HMSO, 1986, para 51.
Beverstock v Dairy Product Packers (1981) IRLR 265 demonstrates the importance of making offences distinct and known to the workforce.
Egg Store Ltd v Leibovic (1977) ICR 260.

Bibliography

This bibliography has been prepared by the Library staff of the Institute's Information and Advisory Services. The working party acknowledges with great thanks the assistance given by library staff in preparing this publication.

Books

ALCOHOL CONCERN. Workplace Advisory Service. *Information pack*. London, Alcohol Concern, 1987, various paging.

ALCOHOL EDUCATION CENTRE. *Guidelines for the formulation of a company alcoholism policy*. London Education Centre, 1978, 12pp.

BEYER Janice M. and TRICE Harrison M. *Implementing change: alcoholism policies in work organizations*. New York, Free Press, 1978, xix, 347pp.

CONFEDERATION OF BRITISH INDUSTRY. *Danger – drugs at work*. London, CBI, 1986, 31pp.

CYSTER Richard, MACKLIN Debbie and McEWEN James. *Alcohol policies: a guide to action at work*. London, Industrial Society, 1987, 46pp.

GRANT Marcus and PLANT Martin. *Drinking and alcohol problems*. London, Wine and Spirit Association of Great Britain, 1978, 40pp.

HEALTH AND SAFETY EXECUTIVE. *The problem drinker at work*. London, HMSO, 1981, 15pp. (Occasional paper series: OP1.)

INCOMES DATA SERVICES LIMITED. *Drink and drugs dismissals*. London, IDS, 1982, 26pp. (Brief supplement, no.36.)

INCOMES DATA SERVICES LIMITED. *Protecting employees' health*. London, IDS, 1986, 23pp. (Study 371.)

INTERNATIONAL LABOUR OFFICE. *Alcohol and drugs: programmes of assistance for workers*. Geneva, International Labour Office, 1987, 243pp. (Conditions of Work Digest, Vol.6, No.1)

JONES Thomas. 'Alcohol and drug dependency'. pp.481-508 in O'DONNELL Michael P. and AINSWORTH Thomas H. *eds*. *Health promotion in the workplace*. New York, Wiley, 1984, xiv, 773pp.

McNEILL Andrew. *Alcohol problems in employment: a British perspective*. London, Institute of Alcohol Studies, 1982, 13pp. (Occasional paper no.1.)

McNEILL Andrew. *Guidelines: alcohol education in the workplace*. London, Institute of Alcohol Studies, 1983, 8pp.

McNEILL Andrew. *Guidelines for managements and trade unions*. London, Institute of Alcohol Studies, 1983, 16pp.

McNEILL Andrew, *Guidelines for occupational health and welfare services*. London, Institute of Alcohol Studies, 1983, 8pp.

McNEILL Andrew. *Guidelines for supervisors*. London, Institute of Alcohol Studies, 1983, 12pp.

NATIONAL COUNCIL ON ALCOHOLISM. *The problem drinker at work*. London, the Council, n.d. 7pp.

SCHRAMM Carl J. *et al*. *Workers who drink: their treatment in an industrial setting*. Lexington, Massachusetts, Lexington Books, 1978, xv, 153pp.

SCHRAMM Carl J., *ed. Alcoholism and its treatment in industry*. Baltimore, Johns Hopkins University Press, 1977, xii, 191pp.
TRADES UNION CONGRESS. *Problem drinking: TUC guidelines for a workplace policy*. London, TUC, 1986, 25pp.
WEISS Richard M. *Dealing with alcoholism in the workplace*. New York, Conference Board, 1980, 59pp.

Articles

HERBERT E. 'Alcohol abuse at work'. *Occupational Safety and Health*. Vo.17, No.7, July 1987. pp18-20.
'Alcohol and drugs'. *Industrial Relations Review and Report*. No.378, October 1986. (Industrial Relations Legal Information Bulletin pp2-8.)
CYSTER R. 'Alcohol and industry: setting the scene'. *British Journal of Administrative Management*. Vol.35, No.8, December 1985/January 1986, pp293-6.
MOLLOY J. 'Alcohol and the OH role: Part 1. The effects of problem drinking'. *Occupational Health*. Vo.35, No.9, September 1983, pp409-18.
MOLLOY J. 'Alcohol and the OH role: Part 2. Prevention of alcoholism'. *Occupational Health*. Vol.35, No.10, October 1983, pp447-57.
MOLLOY J. 'Alcohol and the OH role: Part 3. Restoration of health'. *Occupational Health*. Vol.35, No.11, November 1983, pp507-12.
MORTIMER B. 'Alcohol and work – an explosive cocktail' *Employment Gazette*. Vol.96, No.2, February 1988, pp59-64.
HAMILTON M. 'Alcohol dependence: a different approach'. *Occupational Safety and Health*. Vol.17, No.9, September 1987, pp40-1.
KNOX J. and FENLEY A. 'Alcohol problems at work – some medical and legal considerations'. *Personnel Review*. Vol.14, No.1, 1985, pp32-5.
EMERY M. 'Alcoholism wins the "Black Oscar".' *Occupational Safety and Health*. Vol.9, No.9, September 1979, pp8-9, 11-13.
BEAUMONT P.B. and ALLSOP S.J. 'Beverage report'. *Occupational Safety and Health*. Vol.13, No.10, October 1983, pp25-7. (The relationship between alcohol abuse and industrial accidents.)
'Calling time on problem drinking'. *Bargaining Report*. No.57, December 1986, pp9-13.
'Civil Service alcoholism policy'. *Industrial Relations Review and Report*. No.273, June 1982. (Health and Safety Bulletin pp6-8).
BEAUMONT P.B. 'Company alcohol policies in Scotland'. *Occupational Safety and Health*. Vol.12, No.5, May 1982, pp20-1.
SCHACHTER V. and GEIDT T.E. 'Cracking down on drugs'. *Across the Board*. Vol XXII, No.11, November 1985, pp28-37.
'Dealing with alcoholism in industry'. *Industrial Relations Review and Report*. No.159, September 1977. (Health and Safety Information Bulletin pp1-8).
TWOMEY C. 'Dealing with drink (The need for alcohol policies and employee assistance programmes)'. *Industrial Society*. June 1987, pp30-1.
ALLSOP D.T. 'Dealing with problems of alcohol in an employment setting'. *Health Services Manpower Review*. Vol.12, No.4, February 1987, pp20-2.
RICHARDS A. 'A drain on resources'. *Occupational Safety and Health*. Vol.16, No.3, March 1986, pp40-2.
'Drink and drugs at work'. *Employment Digest*. No.184, 29 July 1985, pp1,8.
O'BROIN C. 'Drink and drugs at the workplace'. *Personnel Management*. Vol.17, No.12, December 1985, pp28-30. (Employee assistance programmes.)

HERBERT E. 'Drug abuse at work'. *Occupational Safety and Health.* Vol.17, No.8, August 1987, pp28-31.

GARDINER A.W. 'Handling alcohol abuse at work: the disciplinary and the coercive alternatives'. *Occupational Health Review.* No.4, December 1986/ January 1987, pp23-4.

APPELBAUM S.H. 'A human resources counselling model: the alcoholic employee'. *Personnel Administrator.* Vol.27, No.8, August 1982, pp35, 37-8, 40-2, 44

HYMAN J. and BEAUMONT P.B. 'Identifying the problem drinker'. *Occupational Safety and Health.* Vol.14, No.11, November 1984, pp26-9.

STEDDON P. 'The juggernaut in the blind spot (drug abuse)'. *Training and Development.* Vol.6, No.7, November 1987, pp.16-17, 19-20, 22.

MADONIA J.F. 'Managerial responses to alcohol and drug abuse'. *Personnel Administrator.* Vol.29, No.6, June 1984, pp134-5, 137-9 (Results of a survey conducted in Los Angeles, 1981.)

BLACKLAWS A. 'Tackling alcoholism'. *Industrial Society.* Vol.61, November/December 1979, pp14-15. (Alcohol policy and programme at Scottish and Newcastle Breweries.)

BENSINGER A. and PILKINGTON C.F. 'Treating chemically dependent employees in a non-hospital setting'. *Personnel Administrator.* Vol.30, No.8, August 1985, pp45-6, 50-2.

'Unfair dismissal and drinking'. *Industrial Relations Review and Report.* No.171, March, 1978. (Legal Information Bulletin pp1-6.)

BEAUMONT P. 'Unions, organization change and alcohol policy'. *Industrial Relations Journal.* Vol.14, No.3, Autumn 1983, pp68-75.